BRITAIN 1970-2020

Pat Thane

Gretton Books

Cambridge

Pat Thane

First published in 2024 by Gretton Books

© Pat Thane 2024

A CIP catalogue record for this title is available from the British Library.

ISBN   978-1-7399497-4-7

Printed and bound by 4edge in the UK

CONTENTS

Pat Thane

Introduction 1945-1970

Great Britain, its official title, includes England, Wales and Scotland. Wales was united with England in 1542, Scotland joined them in 1707. In 1801 they were joined by Ireland, forming the United Kingdom of Great Britain and Ireland, until in 1922 the independent Irish Free State was founded in Ireland alongside six of the nine Ulster counties. The title changed again to United Kingdom of Great Britain and Northern Ireland (UK). Despite their long union there were always real differences dividing England, Scotland and Wales. Nationalist movements grew gradually in Wales and Scotland from the early twentieth century. Wales, the smallest country, with a population of 2,740,300 in 1971, 3,108, 000 in 2021 shared the English political, administrative and legal systems until devolution in 1999 and had few independent powers, but was proud to preserve and develop its distinctive cultural features, in particular its language. The population of England was 45,880,000 in 1971, 56,500, 000 in 2021 with considerable regional diversity, especially between north and south and between big cities and elsewhere. Scotland had 5,229,000 people in 1971, 5,480,000[1] in 2021 and retained separate legal and judicial systems from its time of independence, a different local administrative structure from England and Wales, and a separate established church, the Presbyterian Church of Scotland. It provided high standards of education for the whole population earlier than England, with a different structure of state, including university, education. The Scottish language, Scots Gaelic, was/is less widely used than Welsh, but Scots have also retained a firm sense of their cultural distinctiveness.

In the UK the 1970s has a reputation for conflict and decline after thirty years of unity and progress since 1945.[2] The reality was less dramatic and desolate, except in Northern Ireland where the conflict was real. There was social and economic progress from 1945 compared with the poverty, inequality and unemployment before the war which returned from the 1980s, though it would be an over-statement to describe the 1940s-1970s as a 'Golden Age' in Britain as it is in some other west European countries. The post-1945 Labour government revived the economy, establishing near full employment for the first time in peacetime, lasting to the 1970s, so successfully that a labour shortage led them in the late 1940s to encourage immigration, first from Europe then from the Commonwealth, increasing the ethnic diversity of the population, and racial tensions. Labour also created a lasting 'Welfare State', providing services and benefits for the whole population, better than anything before, especially the National Health Service (NHS), established in 1948, for the first time providing free health care for all.

But the welfare reforms were more limited than Labour aspired to because it prioritised economic growth as key to higher living standards. Also, it had to pay the costs of the war and continuing defence costs, aiming to retain Britain's international power and status in the Cold War world. This prospect weakened in 1956 when a Conservative Prime Minister, Anthony Eden, allied with France to prevent Egypt nationalising the Suez Canal, which linked both countries with their Asian colonies and trading partners, only to withdraw ignominiously when the UN and US opposed them. As the US Secretary of State, Dean Acheson, put it in 1962 'Great Britain has lost an Empire but has not yet found a role'. Britain indeed experienced, often supported, most of its former colonies gaining independence, sometimes peacefully, sometimes violently as when the Indian subcontinent was rapidly divided in 1947 into two republics, Hindu India and Muslim Pakistan.

Labour hoped to remain in government long enough to complete its welfare state ambitions, but it narrowly lost the 1951 election to the Conservatives. It is sometimes argued that 1945-1970s was a period of 'consensus', agreement on policy issues, between Labour and Conservatives. Disagreement between them was certainly less acute than later in the century but close agreement there was not. Near full employment continued under the Conservatives and living standards continued to rise, but the economy slipped behind its rivals and poverty and inequality grew. The Conservatives cut taxes and some of Labour's economic controls and did little to expand state welfare. Britain's share of world trade declined. By 1961 Prime Minister Harold Macmillan decided that membership of the European Economic Community (EEC, founded in 1958, since 1993 the EU) would rescue the economy, but the President of France, Charles de Gaulle, said 'Non'. He believed the UK was too close to the US to be a loyal European nation.

Labour returned to government in 1964, led by Harold Wilson. It aimed to complete the Welfare State and further modernise the economy but was held back by inheriting an unexpectedly large budget deficit from what it called the 'thirteen wasted years' of Conservative government, and later by financial crises. Labour set out to grow the economy with improved management training and by funding research and development in new technology, including computing and electronics. Some still saw joining the EEC as essential to further development, but de Gaulle again refused, despite Wilson keeping his distance from the US to reassure the Europeans. Yet, despite financial problems, Labour introduced lasting social and cultural changes. It replaced the socially selective secondary schools with comprehensives and increased the numbers and quality of affordable council housing. In a remarkable succession of reforms, it was the first country in western Europe to legalise abortion, it partially decriminalised homosexuality, eased divorce and access to birth control, building upon and promoting a more sexually open culture, condemned by some as creating a 'permissive society'. It also abolished capital punishment and introduced the first legislation for gender equality in pay and against race discrimination. But Labour had again achieved less than it hoped when it lost the 1970 election to the Conservatives, after a campaign in which they faced racist attacks.

1970-1979

The Conservatives were now led by Edward Heath. His decidedly non-consensual programme, announced before the election, included restricting trade union rights to strike and shifting social security benefits, including pensions and sickness insurance, from the universality (i.e., available to the whole population in return for compulsory contributions) introduced in 1946 to means-testing, or 'selectivity' as he preferred to call it, confining benefits to people on low incomes, funded by taxes. He proposed to reduce taxes, abolish controls on wages and prices and liberate business from government 'shackles'. Heath was as committed as Wilson to improving Britain's economic competitiveness, but by very different means. He believed in only very limited state intervention when unavoidable to assist growth in a predominantly free enterprise economy. He had the advantage of inheriting from Labour a large surplus of revenue over spending commitments, while criticising Labour for excessive spending.

Heath's government abolished Labour's subsidies to economic development areas and industrial modernisation, then hit problems. In 1971 Rolls-Royce, Britain's internationally prestigious manufacturer of aero engines and luxury cars, faced bankruptcy. It was too important to lose and the government felt forced to nationalise it. The car manufacturing arm was privatised again in 1973. Also in 1971, a leading Glasgow shipbuilding firm, Upper Clyde Shipbuilders (UCS), verged on bankruptcy. It had been formed by Labour in 1968 from a merger of smaller firms, with substantial grants and loans, to revive a flagging industry. It was recovering well until the Conservatives withdrew support in 1971, threatening extensive unemployment. The government refused to save it until trade unions adopted the unusual tactic of a 'work-in', keeping the yards working without pay, for a strike would destroy the business. They received favourable national and international publicity, support and finance from Glasgow City Council, Scottish churches, Scottish businessmen, who had much to lose if it collapsed, and John Lennon of the Beatles. In 1972 the government felt forced to take it into partial government ownership again with a grant of £35m, handing its management to an American firm convinced of its viability. It then operated successfully.

The government was concerned about unemployment heading, for the first time since 1947, towards the symbolically important one million. The Bretton Woods system of fixed exchange rates linked to the US dollar, pegged to the value of gold, which helped stabilise the international economy from its establishment in 1944, collapsed when the US withdrew in 1971, and the pound slipped badly. The government tried to increase demand by cutting taxes. When that failed, they resorted to funding public works including road building, subsidising industry and controlling prices, while interest rates were cut to encourage borrowing and spending. Trade unions demanded substantial pay rises to cope with rising prices. Strikes increased, with widespread public support; trade union membership, already at its highest ever level, rose steadily. Coal-miners struck in a nationalised industry. Mining was declining as oil replaced coal as a source of power. Its workforce shrank from over 700,000 in 1961 to under 300,000 in 1971, and wages fell. After six weeks of the strike, the government declared a state of emergency, placed industry on a three-day week to conserve power and established an enquiry under a leading judge. With remarkable speed, after two days this endorsed the workers' demands due to the industry's importance to the economy and the harsh working conditions. The government backed down again and conceded an average 17% pay rise. It then froze pay, prices, rents, and dividends for the rest of its time in office, achieving lower inflation, higher output and lower unemployment.

The economic problems fuelled racism, as immigrants were unfairly blamed for taking British jobs and abusing benefits. In response the government introduced the Commonwealth Immigration Act, 1971, which added further restrictions to those introduced by Conservatives in 1962 to the rights of Commonwealth citizens to remain in Britain. It was now limited to British passport-holders and people whose parents or grand-parents - or those of their husband, but not their wife - were native-born British subjects, effectively excluding most people of colour. However, in

1973 the government accepted more than 20,000 desperate Ugandan Asians fleeing President Idi Amin's brutal Africanisation drive.

Heath hoped for economic revival when the UK finally joined the EEC in January 1973. He was strongly committed to Europe and unusually cool among British leaders towards the US. Georges Pompidou had now replaced de Gaulle as President of France and supported UK entry, which divided the two main British political parties. Then in late 1973 came an international 'oil shock', as Middle East oil producers cut supplies to supporters of Israel in the Arab-Israeli war of October 1973, including the UK, causing a severe crisis. UK oil prices doubled, causing inflation, and the government declared another three-day week. Other, stronger, well-managed economies, as in France and Germany, handled the crisis better. UK miners took advantage of the boost to their bargaining power as coal again became essential and started another strike in February 1974. Heath called an election, declaring the main issue was 'Who Governs Britain?', government or the unions? But voters were more concerned about the three-day week, power cuts, petrol shortages, inflation and the budget deficit. Conservative 'free enterprise' was not working. Also, low-paid workers felt disadvantaged by cuts to social security payments and fewer council houses built as the government reduced subsidies to local authorities and raised rents.

A further crisis arose from conflict between Catholics and Protestants in Northern Ireland which had started in 1968. Catholics, inspired by the current Black American civil rights movement, protested about discrimination in work, housing and much else, in a province controlled by Protestants. Conflict intensified, especially when in 1972 British troops, installed to quell violence, shot and killed thirteen Catholics on a peaceful

7

protest march in Derry. The 'Troubles', as they became known, continued for thirty years of violence. Heath's failure to resolve the crisis, combined with the other difficulties, counted against him. Britain was clearly divided, especially over economic matters. In the February 1974 election Labour, still led by Harold Wilson, won most seats but fewer votes than the Conservatives and no overall majority. Heath tried to hang on, but the Liberals refused a coalition and Labour returned to government with limited power.

Labour settled the miners' strike with a 29% pay rise, ended pay controls, the three-day week and restrictions on strike action introduced by the Conservatives. Income tax, paid by few manual workers at this time, rose, basic foods were subsidised, council rents frozen and subsidies increased for local authority council house building. Inflation continued to rise internationally to exceptional levels (17% in UK in September 1974), but earnings outstripped prices and Wilson judged it safe to call another election in October 1974. He won an overall majority of three seats. Before the election, he agreed to the demands of Labour left-wingers to hold a referendum on EEC membership. They believed it was too capitalist, free-market oriented. Right-wing Conservatives also opposed membership because they believed it betrayed Britain's obligations to the Commonwealth, though in 1975 all 34 Commonwealth nations signed a communique stating that Britain's continued membership was in their best interests. The argument to remain in the EEC stressed that close ties to a successful economic unit strengthened the economy and secured Britain's world role. Wilson himself was divided. In 1975 remaining in the EEC gained 67.2% of votes, exiting 32.8%, on a 67.5% turnout across the

UK. All four countries returned clear majorities for membership, but the debate continued.[3]

Labour returned to the mission of reversing the relative decline of British manufacturing and trade, including subsidising and seeking to modernise the failing motor industry, without great success. It national-ised British Aerospace in 1977 and the British National Oil Corporation in 1976 following the welcome discovery of oil in the North Sea, revitalised electronics and financed further advances in computer technology. But older established manufacturing continued to decline, suffering from the lack of consensus or consistent planning and support for research, innovation and training between governments of different political persuasions compared with successful rivals such as Germany, and lacking support from the flourishing financial sector which preferred to invest overseas. Unemployment passed one million for the first time since 1947, reaching 1.4m in January 1976, mainly in traditional manufacturing and mining areas. Inflation reached 20%. Labour avoided serious industrial conflict in these hard times for workers through wage agreements with the unions and in 1976 established the Advisory, Conciliation and Arbitration Service (ACAS), a stronger version of existing government provision for settling disputes. Women workers gained rights already prevalent in the EEC, including statutory maternity leave, and it became illegal to dismiss a woman because she was pregnant, though it continued. The unemployed were assisted by adequate, though not generous, benefits.

In March 1976 Wilson unexpectedly retired. It was later revealed that he was suffering from the early stages of dementia. The Foreign Secretary, James Callaghan, was elected by Labour MPs to succeed him, defeating left-winger Michael Foot. Callaghan was a moderate centrist. But Labour declined in the polls and lost its majority following by-election defeats, hit by inflation, unemployment and criticism from an increasingly right-wing press. It survived through a pact with the Liberals and by promising progress towards devolved powers to the growing movements of Welsh and Scottish nationalism. But the pound declined in value and the deficit grew despite spending cuts. The Chancellor, Denis Healey, was persuaded by the Treasury in 1976 that the deficit was so great he should take the unprecedented step of requesting a loan from the International Monetary Fund (IMF), which further weakened the pound. The UK was the first major economy to request a loan from the IMF and it was the largest it had given, $39bn. Healey made further spending cuts mainly to housing and education and sold part of the government's majority shareholding in British Petroleum (BP), which was very active in the North Sea. Healey later revealed that the Treasury had 'grossly overestimated' the deficit and the loan was unnecessary. He only drew on half, and it was fully repaid before Labour left office in 1979, most of the cuts were restored and the economy recovered. The pound rose in value, assisted by increasing North Sea oil output. The balance of payments achieved a £1bn surplus in 1978, inflation fell to 8%, and trade grew. But the good news was little known at the time, or since, and right-wing politicians and the press continued to pillory Labour over the loan and their supposed bad financial management. In fact, it was better than that of successive Conservative governments, but the onslaught damaged Labour politically.[4]

It was also little known, then or since, that under this government the post-war welfare state reached its peak of services and benefits, and the gap between low and high incomes was the narrowest of the century. From 1974 Labour for the first time raised pensions and other allowances annually in line with earnings or prices, whichever was higher. In 1975 it introduced State Earnings Related Pensions (SERPS), a major improvement on the existing flat-rate pension which it supplemented, bringing UK pensions closer to standards elsewhere in the EEC. It gave much improved pension rights to women and unpaid carers. There were growing numbers of low-income families headed by single mothers, as more couples divorced or separated in 'permissive' Britain, and women's work and pay opportunities remained weak. Following a comprehensive report in 1974 on the many disadvantages of one-parent families by a committee established by Labour in 1969, and pressure from campaigners including the Child Poverty Action Group (CPAG) and the expanding Women's Liberation Movement (WLM), in 1976 a Child Benefit was introduced for children of single parents. A larger benefit was extended to all children in 1979, replacing the inadequate family allowances introduced in 1946. This followed the revelation in 1965 of unexpectedly high levels of poverty under the Conservatives, affecting 2.5 million children due to low parental incomes, known as 'the rediscovery of poverty', which sparked the campaigns.[5]

Fewer homes were built, but fewer were needed and improvement grants and mortgage subsidies introduced by Labour in the mid-1960s enabled renovation of sound older houses by councils and 'gentrification' of previously decaying inner-city areas by middle-class owner-occupiers, in place of clearance and re-building. Between 1971 and 1981 the number of homes in England without a bath or shower fell from 1.6m to 0.5m, those lacking an indoor toilet from 2m to 0.6m, and without hot water supply to the kitchen from 2.4m to 0.7m.[6] Homelessness fell, especially after 1977 when Labour required local authorities to house the unintentionally homeless. It increased funding of the NHS, especially for poorer districts, a persistent problem of inequality which declined but did not disappear.

The service sector and white-collar jobs in the public and private sectors expanded while manual work declined, encouraging mobility from the working into the middle classes, assisted by improved educational opportunities. With the introduction of comprehensive schools more children stayed at school to later ages, more gained qualifications and more entered higher education as universities and polytechnics gradually expanded, though universities still admitted more middle-class, male and white students. For the well-paid, consumption grew despite inflation. Central heating spread, there was more eating out in a wider international range of restaurants and more people enjoyed overseas holidays. Despite the dismal reputation of the 1970s as a time of decline and strife, persistently promoted by Conservatives into the next century, blaming Labour and the unions, the thinktank the New Economics Foundation concluded from surveys in 2004 that 1976 was widely felt to be Britain's best year since the 1950s.[7] Meanwhile, free market ideas, increasingly labelled Neoliberalism, were spreading internationally, challenging left of centre governments, assisted in Britain by the growth of a strident right-wing popular press.[8]

Trade union membership reached its peak of the century in 1979, 50% of the workforce, 13m workers. Growth was greatest among white-collar workers, especially in the public sector, among women, a high proportion of whom worked in the public sector, and Black, Asian and minority ethnic workers who were generally lower-paid and increasingly supported by unions. In 1976 a widely supported strike by Asian women about pay and conditions at Grunwick, a photo-processing business in London, publicised race and gender discrimination at work, but after three years it was unsuccessful. As in other private sector businesses, militant workers faced intransigent opposition from an employer who refused to recognise the union, part of the rising international neoliberal tide. Meanwhile unions and many others supported the increasingly active international movement against apartheid, White dominance, in mainly Black South Africa. In 1978 the Union of Postal Workers refused to handle mail for South Africa, which was illegal, but Labour took no action, consistent with government and Commonwealth agreements to impose sanctions on South Africa.

Strikes increased, including among essential but low-paid public sector workers such as ambulance drivers, refuse collectors and school caretakers. The government had imposed pay controls on the public sector to restrain spending. Militancy among such workers was so rare that it suggests their desperation, especially due to continuing high prices. The right-wing press, most stridently the *Sun,* shrieked about a 'winter of discontent' as strikes grew in 1978/79, causing, they claimed, shortages of food and medical supplies, illustrated with images of cancer-stricken children, unburied bodies in cemeteries and rubbish piled in streets. Union leaders pointed out that essential supplies always got through, 98% of establishments had no dispute in 1977-1979 and more days were lost through sickness and accident than strikes. But this made little impact and Labour suffered in opinion polls. The government, rather reluctantly, agreed a settlement with the Trades Union Congress (TUC) including substantial pay rises, without the disastrous consequences forecast by the media. Inflation fell in 1978/79 and the economy stabilised, though the long-term problems of declining manufacturing and trade and poor productivity remained.

Trade unionists were not the only people fighting in the 1970s to reduce inequalities and improve living and working conditions for themselves and others. Exceptional numbers of mainly younger people collaborated on issues of gender, race and sexual preference, choosing what was later called 'identity politics' over more traditional political organisations, though not always rejecting them. Gender inequalities were challenged by feminists in the WLM, formed in 1969. Women had never stopped campaigning for gender equality since demanding and getting the vote earlier in the century, but they became internationally more active from the late 1960s as more women were educated, independent and impatient with their limited opportunities. The WLM was an organisation mainly of white, middle-class women, but Black and Asian women's groups increasingly emerged to challenge the restrictive immigration laws and the double discrimination they experienced due to race and gender.[9]

In 1975 Labour passed a Sex Discrimination Act, partly in response to WLM campaigns, partly business left over from their last period of government, partly adopting the practices of the EEC. It outlawed discrimination in employment, education and provision of housing, goods or services. At last married women no longer needed their husband's permission to undertake any financial arrangement even when they had independent earnings; they could even have their own bank accounts. An Equal Opportunities Commission (EOC) was established to investigate complaints and support women claiming discrimination. The Act forced medical schools to remove the quotas strictly limiting women students, and by the early 1990s over 50% of medical students were women. The proportion of female lawyers rose from 4% in 1971 to 27% in 1990. Most previously all-male Oxford and Cambridge colleges admitted women for the first time, and the number of women students, previously in female-only colleges, rose from 15% and 10% respectively to over 50% in the 1990s.

More women, including mothers, entered employment, though still concentrated in lower-paid, lower-status, often part-time, work; the workforce remained strongly gender-divided. Childcare was scarce and expensive and still generally seen as the mother's responsibility. Gender roles in marriage shifted very slowly. The Equal Pay Act, 1970, came fully into force in 1975: the average gender pay gap narrowed only from about 50% to 40% between 1970 and 1980. Women's opportunities were constrained by continuing limitations on their education. More girls than boys left school without qualifications, though the female proportion of university students rose from 28% in 1971 to 38% in 1979, concentrated in arts and social sciences with few in sciences or engineering. They remained the great majority of students in two-year teacher-training colleges. More older women attended university as mature students, especially the Open University, established by Harold Wilson in 1969 to extend opportunities.

The WLM and others brought to public notice issues that were previously hidden or overlooked, including domestic violence, which was by no means new but ignored by police and the courts. Women campaigned about this, opened refuges to enable victims and their children to escape violent partners and demanded legal reform. By 1980 there were about 200 refuges. The Domestic Violence and Matrimonial Proceedings Act, 1976, made domestic violence a specific offence for the first time; violent partners could be punished and excluded from the family home. From 1977 local authorities were obliged to house women made homeless by domestic violence, but it did not stop, and police still did not always take it seriously. The WLM also raised awareness of rape, another long-standing form of violence rarely publicly discussed and not always treated seriously by police or the courts, who often blamed the victim. Again, feminists established refuges and counselling centres and the Sexual Offences (Amendment) Act, 1976, guaranteed anonymity in court for victims, removing an obstacle to their coming forward. It was another advance, but rapes did not diminish and still were not always taken seriously by the justice system. There was no gender revolution in the 1970s, but a continuation of gradual, incomplete gains in women's opportunities and legal protections which had been progressing since early in the century.

Gay men and increasingly, though separately, women also organised, from 1970 as the Gay Liberation Front (GLF), following the partial decrim-inalisation of homosexuality in 1967. They established counselling and befriending services and helplines and campaigned for greater social rights and social acceptability, becoming visible after centuries of secrecy with public events like Gay Pride marches which began in 1972. The GLF supported women's, anti-racist and trade union campaigns, including supporting the miners in 1974 with a 'Pits and Perverts' campaign which miners appeared to welcome. There were smaller, quieter transgender campaigns and society gradually became more open, but homophobia and transphobia persisted, with murders of gay men.

Heterosexual behaviour also changed, continuing the 'permissiveness' believed, not wholly accurately, to have been born in the 1960s. Behaviour had been gradually changing over several decades. Divorce became easier following reform in 1969 and shot up, marriage rates fell, and more unmarried couples openly lived together and had children. Births declined as the birth pill, introduced in the 1960s, eased birth control and more women aimed for careers.[10] There were increasing numbers of openly gay households, male and female, and complex families of divorced and re-partnered parents, accepted by many but not by all.[11] 'The moral structure of two thousand years of civilisation is collapsing' declared the *Daily Mail* in 1971.

Another focus of activism and cultural change in the 1970s concerned race. Second generation immigrants, children of migrant parents, were reaching adulthood and experiencing racism, restricted opportunities, unemployment, and police aggression. They promoted distinctive cultural identities, including through events like the Notting Hill carnival, established in 1976 by people of Caribbean origin, modelled on Trinidad carnivals, and run annually ever since before large multi-racial crowds. Also in 1976, black and white youth united in Rock Against Racism (RAR), running events where black and white bands played under anti-racist banners; they played 200 very popular concerts in their first year. It was part of a wider rise to prominence of youth culture, influencing entertainment and fashion as well as politics since the 1950s and 1960s. Not all young, or older, people were anti-racist. Some joined the racist National Front, formed in 1967, but it gained few votes in the elections of 1970

and 1974 and soon declined into insignificance. In 1976 Labour introduced a Race Relations Act, extending its previous anti-discrimination
legislation to include employment, training, education and provision of
goods and services, and it became an offence to incite racial hatred. It
established the Commission for Racial Equality (CRE) to investigate cases
of discrimination and assist individuals taking cases to court, following
pressure from anti-racist organisations and the growing number repres-
enting Black, Asian and minority ethnic communities, including the
Campaign Against Racial Discrimination, the West Indian Standing
Committee, and the Indian Workers Committee, which increasingly co-
operated with one another.

In 1977 the Anti-Nazi League (ANL) was formed, mainly by white
activists with Black, Asian and minority ethnic support. It had wide
support from professionals, trade unionists, entertainers, sports stars,
and people of all ages. With RAR it organised demonstrations and events:
the first concert attracted 80,000 people. Some, mainly Labour-led, local
councils supported their minority ethnic communities. But still few Black
or Asian people rose above the level of skilled manual work, including in
1974 one-fifth of Black, Asian or minority ethnic men with university
degrees (unthinkable for white male graduates), except in the NHS, which
has always depended upon doctors and nurses of Asian, African, and
Caribbean origin. Many Asians were self-employed in small shops and
restaurants. Ethnic minorities generally lived in segregated areas of towns
and cities with poor amenities; very few gained council houses.[12] But the
minority group suffering most discrimination had long been Gypsies and
Travellers. Following an investigation in 1976, Labour introduced 100%
grants for local authorities to build secure sites for caravans, but they still

experienced poor access to health care, education, and other services and much discrimination.[13]

Another important change in the 1970s was the continued growth of nationalism and demands for independence in Wales and Scotland, indicated by the gradually growing success of the Nationalist parties, Plaid Cymru and the Scottish National Party (SNP), in parliamentary elections. They gained three and eleven seats respectively in October 1974. Nationalism was driven by declining mining and manufacture in both countries, since both had long been central to their economies, creating unemployment and the desire to control their own economic development. In 1969 Labour appointed a Commission which in 1973 recommended elected assemblies for both countries. After extended, tense parliamentary discussions it was agreed in 1978 to hold referenda on devolution of powers, requiring a minimum 40% of each electorate to vote 'Yes'. Referenda were held on 1 March 1979. Scotland narrowly voted 'Yes' but by too small a majority to gain devolution, while 46.9% of Welsh electors voted 'No' and 11.9% 'Yes'.[14] Meanwhile the 'Troubles' in Northern Ireland became increasingly violent, worsened by rising unemployment especially among Catholics, spreading into fatal bomb attacks by the Irish Republican Army (IRA) in Britain. In October 1974 five people were killed by a bomb in a pub in Guildford, Surrey, in November further pub bombings killed two in Woolwich, London, twenty-one in Birmingham. Repeated attempts by the UK government to negotiate a settlement failed, while it directly controlled an administration rendered dysfunctional by the conflict.

A general election was unavoidable in 1979. Labour was undermined as much by the outcomes of the referenda as by the 'winter of discontent' when the Scottish National Party (SNP) MPs supported a Conservative No-Confidence Motion which the government lost by one vote. The election was held in May. The Conservatives, now led by Margaret Thatcher, made much of the 'winter of discontent' with a prominent poster of a lengthy dole queue captioned 'Labour Isn't Working'. They won by 339 seats to 269, most in prosperous southern England, while Labour won in declining areas of northern England, Scotland and Wales. In 1980 Callaghan resigned and was replaced by Michael Foot, who narrowly defeated Healey to lead a deeply divided party.

1979-90, The 'Iron Lady'

Margaret Thatcher was the UK's first female Prime Minister which some saw as progress towards gender equality. But she was explicitly anti-feminist and hostile to the WLM, which dwindled when it could achieve little change in the face of her antagonism. She appointed only one woman to the Cabinet, briefly, in her eleven years in office. In 1979 just nineteen women were elected among 635 MPs, eight Conservative, eleven Labour. Thatcher was a passionate neoliberal. She aimed, as she put it, to 'roll back the state' as it had developed since 1945, convinced that state welfare discouraged hard work and state intervention crippled the economy. She believed the EEC encouraged state control and, having supported entry in 1973, was increasingly hostile to it. She preferred alliance with the US, especially when Republican Ronald Reagan replaced Democrat Jimmy Carter as President in 1980. She especially valued the alliance against what she described as the 'Communist menace', which she virulently opposed as the Cold War raged. In return, Soviet propaganda labelled her 'the Iron lady'. In 1980 she bought expensive Trident nuclear missiles from the US and US Cruise missiles were stationed in Britain and other NATO countries as 'deterrents' against Russian attack. Labour opposed both, the Campaign for Nuclear Disarmament (CND), founded in 1958, leapt in membership and a women's peace camp was established outside the US missile base at Greenham Common, Berkshire. It remained, mounting repeated demonstrations, until the missiles were removed in 1991 when the USSR was declining and the Cold War melting.

Thatcher severely cut the civil service which she thought too entrenched in the status quo, appointing instead often more expensive policy advisers from business or universities who shared her views. Most of the industries nationalised by Labour after 1945 were gradually privatised. Strict controls were imposed upon trade unions as punishment for their previous 'subversion' and membership and strikes declined. Meanwhile, unemployment rose from 1.2m in May 1979 to 3.2m in January 1983, by far the highest level since the 1930s, as manufacturing and mining continued to decline without government support. Five thousand factories closed 1979-1982. Economic growth was only 0.6% in 1980-83, well below the 2.4% average since 1950, much lower than rival economies, especially Germany. Income tax was cut most on highest incomes, and Value Added Tax (VAT) on spending was raised, hitting low earners hardest. Poverty rose persistently, by 1990 also to the highest levels since the 1930s.[15] Child poverty rose from 8% of all UK children in 1979 to 28% in 1992. Average real incomes rose 37%, 1979-92, but those of the poorest fell 18% while the richest 10% became 61% richer.[16] Thatcher believed that inequality was desirable because it created incentives to hard work.

Poverty rose partly because state welfare was cut. The Housing Act, 1980, gave council tenants the right to buy their homes for 33%-50% below the market value, later raised to 70% in some areas. Sales had always been possible but at market rates and at the discretion of local authorities who could use the proceeds for local needs, powers they now lost. Following pressure from the responsible Minister, Michael Heseltine, initially they could keep three-quarters of the income from sales to build new housing, but this right was eroded when Heseltine was moved to the Ministry of Defence in 1983 and council house building slumped. Sales were popular with buyers, who Thatcher hoped would vote Conservative, but led to a long-term shortage of affordable housing. Council homes shrank from almost one-third to one-fifth of housing 1979-1994. Housing was the area of government spending which dropped furthest. Increasingly it funded non-profit housing associations to meet the need for what was now termed 'social' housing, but their resources were limited, and they were only partially successful in meeting need. Local authority funds were cut, and they raised rents for remaining council tenants to fill the gap. Demand for private rentals grew, but rent controls, in existence since 1915, were abolished in 1988, leading to further increases in rents and stress for people on low incomes. So much so that in 1982/83 the government introduced a means-tested Housing Benefit to assist them, at considerable public cost. Homelessness rose, with increasing numbers of 'rough sleepers' in streets; numbers were always hard to estimate but by 1990 the situation was desperate enough for the government to increase the supply of publicly funded hostel and bed-and-breakfast accommodation.

Social security benefits were severely cut. Thatcher encouraged the rhetoric in some of the popular press that 'welfare' - now a term of disparagement as it had not previously been in Britain - only encouraged 'idleness...cheating... and family breakdown'.[17] Applicants increased, mainly due to involuntary unemployment. From 1983 sickness pay was no longer paid from public funds but by employers, who were expected to eliminate the fake claims assumed but never proven to prevail. The value of pensions and other benefits fell as they were uprated annually in line with prices not earnings, so rose by less, increasing poverty and pension-ers' need for means-tested supplements. In Thatcher's second term, in 1986, there were further cuts. Universal Child Benefit was frozen and supplemented by means-tested Family Credit for low-income families. Discretionary payments for essential items such as clothing and furniture, introduced in 1948, were replaced by loans. Labour's SERPS pension scheme was amended, becoming less generous especially for those with low earnings, while workers were incentivised to take out private pensions which were often so disadvantageous that the post-1997 Labour government paid large sums in compensation. Despite the cuts, govern-ment social security spending rose from £49.9bn pa in 1979/80 to £61.4bn in 1990/91, due to the high administrative costs of the means-tested benefits and increased demand due to poverty among the unemployed and growing numbers of single-parent families. Those in poverty rose from about 5m living below the internationally accepted poverty measure of incomes below 60% of the national median in 1980 to over 11m in 1990.

Labour's legislation requiring local authorities to introduce compre-hensive schools was repealed, but few authorities re-introduced selective schools. By 1995-96 only 5% of UK secondary school pupils attended grammar schools, most in Northern Ireland. From 1980 the government funded means-tested places at independent schools, eventually 35,000 places. Seven per cent of all pupils attended these schools.

Internationally, in Thatcher's first year a long conflict over independence in Rhodesia was settled. An armed struggle for political rights for the Black majority, led by Robert Mugabe, was resisted by the White minority, whose leader, Ian Smith, in 1965 made a Unilateral Declaration of Independence (UDI) preserving White political control. This was opposed by the Labour government and the Commonwealth, who imposed sanctions on Rhodesia. In December 1979 a meeting in London of Commonwealth leaders, advised by the UK Foreign Secretary, Lord Carrington, achieved a settlement and Black majority rule. In 1980 Mugabe was elected President with a landslide victory in what was now Zimbabwe. Thatcher was unenthusiastic but was persuaded by Carrington. She had little interest in the Commonwealth, which distanced her from Queen Elizabeth II, its devoted Head.

Then another Commonwealth crisis arose. The Falkland Islands are among a group of small nations within the former British Empire known as 'British/UK Overseas Territories', self-governing, with the British monarch as head of state, and their populations are full British citizens. The Falklands are in the South Atlantic, close to Argentina which has long claimed them. In April 1982 Argentina, led by right-wing dictator, General Leopoldo Galtieri, invaded. The 1,850 islanders made clear that they preferred distant, benign British rule to the Argentine dictatorship and the British navy was dispatched to defend them. After two months and substantial casualties on both sides Argentina surrendered. Thatcher revelled in the victory, especially because her support had been declining in the polls due to the economic problems, declaiming 'Great Britain is Great again!' Her popularity soared in the polls. Michael Foot supported the war and self-determination for the Falklanders against the Galtieri dictatorship, though many Labour supporters opposed the 'imperialist war'.

But, to the Queen's annoyance, Thatcher hardly protested in 1983 when the US invaded Grenada, a Commonwealth country in the Caribbean, because it had elected a left-wing government which was overthrown. She showed more interest in discussing the future of Hong Kong which was due to revert to Chinese control in 1997 under a Treaty of 1842. She reluctantly agreed to recognise 'one country, two systems', the solution China proposed, theoretically preserving Hong Kong's existing political system. She could not prevent China's potentially authoritarian rule.

In 1983 she faced another election. The Falklands victory benefited her less than is sometimes thought. She won over 600,000 fewer votes than in 1979, but more seats, mainly because the Labour Party had split. Following years of division between left and right, former Home Secretary and President of the EEC, Roy Jenkins, led the breakaway Social Democratic Party (SDP) from 1981. It divided the Labour vote in elections in 1983 and 1987 but won few seats. After the 1983 defeat Foot resigned and was replaced by moderate Neil Kinnock.

The government now cut its subsidies to the declining, still national-ised, coal industry and proposed pit closures as oil prices fell. The National Union of Mineworkers (NUM) had a new, militant president, Arthur Scargill, who called a national strike in 1984. The government subsidised police protection of collieries during picketing, leading to violent episodes. Again, there was substantial public sympathy for the strike, but the coal industry was much weaker than in 1974 and the government more determined. The strike lasted a year until privation drove many miners back to work. The NUM was bankrupted by court rulings against mass picketing, made illegal by Conservative legislation. Pit closures accelerated; by 1994 there were only 11,000 miners in the UK. Hostile employers, legislation and unemployment caused further decline in total union membership. Thatcher had successfully crippled 'the enemy within' as she called unions. Unemployment continued to rise, to at least 3.4m in 1986, probably more since the government repeatedly altered the basis of the statistics to minimise them. It became more difficult to qualify for unemployment benefit as the system was cut back.

The Northern Ireland Troubles deepened as it suffered even greater unemployment than the rest of the UK. They hit the government lethally in October 1984 when the IRA bombed a hotel in Brighton where Thatcher and colleagues were staying for the annual party conference. Five people were killed, including one MP and the wife of another; more than thirty were injured. Thatcher narrowly escaped injury and gave an undaunted speech next day. Five people received long sentences for the bombing. This followed the bomb that killed the Queen's cousin, Earl Mountbatten, on holiday in Sligo in 1979, the deaths of many residents of Northern Ireland and soldiers, bombs that killed three and injured forty-one in London in 1981, then further London bombings and deaths in 1982 and 1983. Despite attempts by the British and Irish governments to negotiate a settlement and, with the US, to provide subsidies for social and economic development in Northern Ireland, violence continued throughout Thatcher's premiership.[18]

Meanwhile, rolling back the 'socialist state' by imposing greater control by the neoliberal state continued. In 1986 the largest local authority in the UK, the Greater London Council (GLC), was abolished. It was headed by Labour's Ken Livingstone, and Thatcher opposed its support for radical feminist and anti-racist movements, low transport costs and use of its income to revive London's economy. Also eliminated were the other seven large metropolitan councils, all Labour-controlled. Their powers were taken over by central government, smaller boroughs or new semi-independent 'agencies' (Quasi-Autonomous Non-Governmental Organisations, or Quangos for short). From 1985 private companies were enabled to run public transport, part of a wider process of 'outsourcing' public services to private, profit-making companies.

Like their Conservative predecessors, Thatcher and her leading colleagues aspired to privatise the NHS, though there were always supporters of state welfare, including the NHS, in the parliamentary party. Some, to her annoyance, were even in the Cabinet, though they rarely lasted long. Privatisers were cautious in her first term because the NHS was popular. The 1983 manifesto 'welcome[d] the growth in private health insurance', though it was never extensive or popular. Tax relief was introduced for employer-provided private insurance, while Treasury officials argued that NHS cost-efficiency still compared well with services in other countries. Managers from the private sector were appointed to replace medical professionals, increasing central supervision at consider-able cost and no evident gain in quality. Thatcher was always suspicious of public sector professionals and believed the private sector more efficient. Charges rose for prescriptions and dental and optical care, until dentists thought it hardly worth staying in the NHS and public dental provision dwindled. Hospital cleaning and catering services were 'out-sourced' to private providers and hospital-acquired infections rocketed. Waiting times for treatment grew along with local inequalities in treatment and outcomes, and staff protested about cuts. GP spending was restricted, and use of private medical services encouraged. The government suppressed a report by a committee established by Labour which described in 1980, before the cuts, how people with low incomes, including many in ethnic minorities, had the poorest health and life expectancy due to socio-economic inequalities, which grew worse through the 1980s.[19]

Further cuts to social security focused on Thatcher's commitment to 'preserving' the 'traditional family', discouraging single parenthood and unmarried partnerships, though these rose to unprecedented levels. Births outside marriage rose from 11.5% of all UK births in 1980 to 28% in 1990, 33.6% in 1995, mostly to cohabiting partners. In 1983 leaked government papers described supporting one-parent families as 'subsidising illegitimacy and immorality'. Thatcher believed that family break-up caused the increasing crime rates in the 1980s and referred to 'young girls who deliberately become pregnant in order to jump the housing queue and gain welfare payments'. No evidence was found for either assertion. She was also convinced that 'feckless fathers' carelessly abandoned their partners and children. One of her last acts in govern-ment, the Child Support Act, 1991, sought to deter or punish them by obliging them to pay maintenance for all their children. It was drafted in a hurry with little understanding of the real circumstances of low-income fathers and mothers and proved costly and inefficient.[20]

'Outsourcing' was imposed upon local services as the government strove to cut the funds and power of local authorities, suppressing what it believed was the excessive generosity of Labour-controlled councils. Thatcher refused to subsidise local authority childcare services to discourage mothers from working away from home, as she herself had done, with care of her two children funded by her millionaire husband. From 1983 councils were obliged to make means-tested charges for residential and community care for older and disabled people, which had been discretionary. Councils could afford to run fewer services and they were increasingly outsourced to profit-making companies who raised charges. Services declined while the numbers of older and disabled people in the population grew due to lengthening life expectancy. Low-income families including those headed by single mothers faced demanding childcare costs. Thatcher faced opposition to privatisation and public sector cuts from Secretaries of State for Scotland, Wales and Northern Ireland, which all had a high proportion of public sector jobs and high unemployment. They were ignored.

Privatisation of nationalised businesses increased, often sold at low prices, including British Telecom in 1984, British Airways and airports in 1987. An advertising campaign urged 'ordinary' people to buy low-cost shares in privatised businesses, with some success, in the belief that, like home ownership, it would increase Conservative support. Most privatised companies cut their workforces and raised senior salaries without becoming evidently more efficient. The financial sector expanded as manufacturing declined, benefiting from reduced government regulation, which also enabled more tax evasion. Salaries zoomed: among directors of one major bank from an annual average £45,000 in 1979 to £225,000 in 1986.[21] This was not unusual. Among the wider population use of credit cards and consequent debt also rocketed, along with consumption, including of household goods, clothing and foreign travel. The gap between high and low incomes, after narrowing from 1945 to the 1970s, started long-term widening.

Hoping to gain from these changes, Thatcher called another election in 1987. The Conservatives won fewer seats but retained a majority of 101, benefiting again from Labour's split. Under its new leadership, Labour's vote rose while that of the SDP did not, leading them to merge with the Liberals to form the Liberal Democrat party in 1988. In Scotland and Wales unemployment and economic decline along with resistance to increasing central government control further stimulated nationalism. Conservative support almost halved in both countries while for Labour it increased.

Thatcher was increasingly hostile to Europe which she believed imposed too many controls, as she asserted in a speech in Bruges in 1988. Britain opted out of EEC 'directives' including those regulating working hours and conditions. She saw less need for a united western Europe as Communism declined in the east. She made congenial contact with Mikhail Gorbachev, the new, conciliatory, general secretary of the Soviet Communist Party, and she supported liberal reform in Hungary and Poland. When the Berlin wall fell in 1989, signalling the end of Communism in Europe, she wanted to be seen as supporting it, but she strongly opposed reunification of Germany which she believed was a potentially dangerous rival. She wanted the former communist countries admitted to the EEC to counterbalance Germany. Her relationship with the US deteriorated from 1988 when Reagan was replaced by Republican George W. Bush who supported German unification. Advised by her Chief Economic Adviser, neoliberal academic economist Alan Walters, she disagreed with Chancellor Lawson and Geoffrey Howe, the Foreign Secretary, over joining the new EEC Exchange Rate Mechanism (ERM), designed to stabilise exchange and interest rates. She reluctantly agreed to join in 1990, when Walters had left following disagreement with Lawson, but by then the exchange rate was too high, leading to a sterling crisis two years later.

Her third term brought further changes to the public sector. The Education Reform Act,1988, reduced local authority powers over schools in England and Wales, which could opt out of their control with central government funding if most parents agreed. All schools could control their own budgets. Already, from 1980, councils were no longer required to provide school meals, which disadvantaged poorer families. The government introduced Britain's first National Curriculum for England and Wales. The Scottish education system remained independent and little changed. The National Curriculum specified curriculum content and attainment targets and tests for children aged 7, 11, 14 and 16. Schools were required to provide religious education 'reflecting Britain's Christian character', as the country became increasingly multi-cultural, with growing communities of Muslims, Hindus and other faith groups. The curriculum was compulsory for state schools, limiting teachers' freedom, discretionary for independent schools. Teachers criticised the constraints, confirming Thatcher's conviction of their resistance to change. There was more support for a single General Certificate of Secondary Education

(GCSE) replacing the socially divisive Ordinary (O) levels, for the 'more able', and Certificates of Secondary Education (CSE) for the rest. Exam results were published in league tables of school performance, which tended to increase social selection as house prices rose fastest near schools high in league tables. The changes were not required by declining school performance, which had risen since comprehensives were introduced. In Scotland schools continued to be locally funded and administered and outcomes continued to improve. There was growing concern in England about large class sizes, shortage of books and equipment and the falling real pay and morale, and increasing workload, of teachers. Yet more young people stayed longer at school, perhaps partly due to rising unemployment and increased opportunities of higher education. For the first time girls outperformed boys at all levels of education, as their opportunities for work and further education improved. This was widely interpreted as a 'problem' of under-performance by boys, whereas the previous under-performance of girls had not been. Girls of Black Caribbean origin outperformed boys, children of Indian and Chinese origin outperformed all others on average, including White children. There were major socio-economic inequalities.

The percentage of 18-21-year-olds in Higher Education in Great Britain rose from 12.7% to 20.3% between 1977 and 1991. Female students were above 50% by the mid-1990s. Better-off males and females were over-represented and ethnic minorities were under-represented. University funding was cut, class sizes grew and facilities declined. In 1985 staff at Thatcher's own university, Oxford, refused her an honorary degree because her policies were 'doing deep and systematic damage to the whole public educational system in Britain'. In 1988 previously quite generous student grants were withdrawn and replaced by loans, further disadvantaging low-income students, who were also hit by withdrawal of their right to claim benefits during vacations. The government proposed fees for home students, but these were resisted by Conservative voters. Overseas students paid fees, which rose. In 1988 polytechnic funding was shifted from local to central government.

Growing poverty and declining health and welfare services aroused wide concern, including in the Church of England. In 1985 the Archbishop of Canterbury, Robert Runcie, led a highly critical report, *Faith in the City.* Church-going Thatcher believed the clergy shared the narrow-minded traditionalism of all professionals and ignored them. Anglicans were not the only critics of the government pressing for change. Gay activism revived when HIV/AIDS emerged as a serious pandemic from 1982. Surveys showed that homophobia was gradually declining, but it remained widespread: gay men suffering from AIDS often received inadequate health care and were demonised for spreading a 'gay plague'. Thatcher was reluctant to act, but, as deaths increased and heterosexuals were diagnosed, the government funded an unprecedented £20m health education campaign of leaflets and advertisements to encourage safe sex and dispel misinformation about how the disease was spread. Homophobic discrimination prompted some Labour local authorities to counter it through sex education in schools, caricatured in the press and opposed by Conservatives including Thatcher, reinforcing her resistance to local government. Section 28 of the Local Government Act, 1988, prohibited it, despite gay protests. It further stimulated gay activism.

Gender equality also progressed slowly, against antagonism. Thatcher's hostility to the EEC grew in 1983 when the European Court of

Human Rights (ECtHR) ordered revision of the Equal Pay Act to replace the requirement for equal pay for 'like work' with 'work of comparable value'. It was the outcome of a case brought by women cooks at a Merseyside shipbuilding firm, supported by the EOC, arguing that their work was comparable with that of male painters, engineers and joiners at the company and should be paid equally. The ECtHR was not an EEC institution but was established in 1959 by the Council of Europe which represented most west European countries including the UK, to apply the European Convention on Human Rights based on the principles of the UN Declaration of Human Rights of 1948. Its status was little understood in Britain and Thatcher attacked it as though it was an EEC institution, as did other leading Conservatives for many decades.

Women campaigners increasingly engaged in formal politics, national and local, as more effective than public protests for engaging with a hostile government. Among Scottish Nationalists, women were active on many issues and joined the movement for devolved government, determined to be fully represented in any elected Scottish government. Similar pressures emerged more slowly in Wales where the women's movement was traditionally weaker. Environmental campaigns also grew as knowledge developed about damage to the environment from pollution and climate change and its impact upon health and the economy. There was no evident response from the government.

Racial tensions continued. 1981 brought riots in deprived inner-city areas with substantial Black populations, including Brixton in London, Toxteth in Liverpool and parts of Bristol and Birmingham. They were partly responding to aggressive policing including use of 'stop and search' powers mainly against young Black men, also to the high levels of unemployment and discrimination experienced by Black and Asian people. An official investigation by Lord Justice Scarman acknowledged widespread discrimination and inequality and recommended action including recruitment of more police from ethnic minorities. Partial implementation of his recommendations did not prevent further outbreaks, most seriously in Tottenham, north London, in 1985 where a policeman was killed. The 1981 British Nationality Act further restricted the rights of Commonwealth citizens to British nationality. Anti-racist groups remained active and members of ethnic minorities were more active in formal politics. By the mid-1980s four Labour-controlled London councils were led by people of Afro-Caribbean origin and four Black Labour MPs were elected in 1987. An Asian Conservative MP was elected in 1992, the first since 1906.[22] Gypsies and Travellers made gains from Labour reforms, including access to education, health and welfare, but still lacked secure camping sites and experienced exclusion and police harassment.[23]

Cuts to public services, unemployment and economic problems increased opposition to Thatcher in Britain and in her party. She continued to seek further control of local authorities. A special frustration was their capacity to raise local rates (taxes fixed by the value of each property) to spend as they chose. She first capped the amount they could raise, then abolished rates, replacing them with a 'community charge', a flat-rate tax on all residents of a local authority area regardless of income. It was labelled a 'poll tax' by its many opponents, including in the Conservative party. It became law in 1987, to be implemented in 1990 in England and Wales, 1987 in Scotland, not at all in Northern Ireland, where there were Troubles enough. There were demonstrations against it, and it was widely evaded, as rates had not been. For many people it raised their tax liability at a time of rising prices and financial pressure. Thatcher sank to 21.6% in the Gallup poll in March 1990. Lawson and Howe resigned from the Cabinet; both made hostile speeches in parliament.

Michael Heseltine, who had previously resigned from the Cabinet, challenged her for the leadership in November 1990. There was no great enthusiasm for him but much opposition to her. She failed to win the leadership election outright then was persuaded to resign by ministers who feared she would lose them the next election.[24] John Major, whom she had promoted to Chancellor of the Exchequer, won the vote of MPs to succeed her, probably because he was more emollient and generally acceptable in the party than Heseltine and other aspirants to the role at a divisive time.

1990-97, John Major

Major was the youngest, least experienced premier of the century, born in 1943, from an unprivileged background like Thatcher (a shopkeeper's daughter) and Heath (son of a lady's maid and a carpenter), in his case the son of a music hall performer who later ran a garden business. Unlike Heath and Thatcher, he did not attend university but trained in banking before entering politics, first as a councillor in Lambeth, south London. Unlike Thatcher he was calm and strove to unite the country and the party. He appeared more liberal, though over time his policies seemed hardly distinguishable from hers and there was little sign of an alternative vision. He had a reputation for being dull and grey, with little obvious interest in contemporary cultural change: his first Cabinet was the first since the Conservative governments of 1951-1964 to include no women;

two women were later recruited. He met gay rights campaigners, and in 1991 launched Opportunity 2000 designed to achieve gender balance at all levels of employment by 2000. But little changed and equalities for women and gay people advanced little under his watch.

He tried initially to distance himself from Thatcher's most unpopular policies by relaxing curbs on social spending, including unfreezing then raising Child Benefit. Heseltine, whom he appointed Secretary of State for the Environment to revise the 'poll tax', replaced it in 1993 with the Council Tax, linked to the value of each property. Councils could not set the amounts due as they had with the rating system. These were set by central government, but councils received the income from council tax on domestic properties, while the income from business rates went to central government. This system applied in England, Wales and Scotland but still not in Northern Ireland where local authorities continued, to the present, to levy rates on domestic properties and to set their amount. Councils faced increased control from a former local councillor (Major), some reorganisation of boundaries and further pressure to privatise services. These were widely criticised, and Conservatives continued to lose heavily in local elections, especially in Scotland. In 1991 Major launched the 'Citizen's Charter' setting out standards for local services, with inspectorates, league tables and complaints procedures, but no enforcement processes. There was little evident improvement.[25]

The civil service and its powers continued to contract, with many government services transferred to semi-independent, mostly privatised, 'agencies', controlling their own budgets and staff, with Ministers no longer accountable for their failures. By 1997 this applied to the administration of social security payments, prisons, Child Support and to Her

Majesty's Revenue and Customs (HMRC) responsible for taxation, among others. Performance declined, with riots and break-outs in prisons and a costly shambles at the Child Support Agency. The Benefits Agency lost a series of legal appeals by claimants who had been unfairly dealt with, at considerable cost. Civil servants' morale declined, and resignations grew as they felt their independence and efficiency further eroded.[26]

Central government control of education increased. Polytechnics were removed from local authority control and re-designated as universities in 1992. Further education colleges, which had improved opportunities for low-income people, dwindled in number as funding declined. Teacher training colleges were amalgamated with universities and training extended from two to three years, leading to a degree for the first time. Government control over funding of the previously autonomous universities increased, regular assessment of the quality of teaching and research was introduced, and league tables encouraged. Student numbers rose faster than funding, but the government still dared not alienate voters by introducing fees.

House-building declined further in the public and private sectors. High interest rates and erosion of tax relief for mortgage payments combined with unemployment and inflation caused growing arrears and repossessions. The cost of Housing Benefit soared as rents rose; eligibility was restricted to rents not exceeding local market rents, to prevent exploitation of the system by landlords. More hostels were provided for homeless people, including women fleeing from domestic violence. Higher standards of health care were specified throughout the NHS, but without enforcement mechanisms there was little sign of improvement.

The Child Support Agency aimed to force 'feckless fathers' to pay for children they had deserted, but many could not afford it because they were too low-paid or unemployed or responsible for second families. It was a costly fiasco. Some fathers staged spectacular protests. Ministers reverted to attacking the welfare system for encouraging partnership breakdown, and single mothers for having children just to gain benefits and a council home, which all research denied. Notoriously at the 1992 Conservative conference, Peter Lilley, Secretary of State for Social Security, intoned, in a pastiche of Gilbert and Sullivan, that he 'had a little list' of:

> 'Benefit offenders who I'll soon be rooting out...
> Young ladies who get pregnant just to jump the housing list.
> And dads who won't support the kids of ladies they have kissed.
> And I haven't even mentioned all those sponging socialists...'

He later blamed the rise in violent crime on the growing numbers of fatherless families, supported by some colleagues and the right-wing press, without evidence. In 1996 One Parent Benefit was frozen and abolished for new claimants.

The post-war welfare state was further eroded with more universal benefits replaced by 'targeted' benefits, which were more costly due to the administrative demands of means-testing, and many eligible people in need failed to apply due to pride or because they were unaware of their rights. Previously universal and contributory unemployment benefit was severely restricted, and claimants risked penalties if they failed to find work, even in areas of high unemployment. Conditions for receiving dis-ability benefits were much tightened, causing severe hardship as too many severely disabled people were judged capable of work, leading to further successful appeals which were costly to the government. Disabled people protested against these and other cuts, and for increased protect-ion against discrimination in employment, education and provision of services. The Disability Discrimination Act, 1995, in principle increased protection against discrimination but introduced no enforcement powers. Income inequality continued to increase. Poverty declined slightly, but still by 1997 about 10.4m people had incomes below the standard poverty line, many of them in low-paid work. Top incomes continued to soar and household debt to grow.

Racial tensions continued. In 1993 a Black teenager, Stephen Lawrence, an A-level student who planned to train in architecture, was murdered while standing harmlessly at a bus stop in south London, in a clearly racist attack. The police failed to conduct serious investigations, causing widespread outrage. This and persistent campaigning by Stephen Lawrence's parents led the next, Labour, government to set up an enquiry in 1999 and two men were convicted in 2012. Immigrants became increasingly diverse: fewer from former colonies, more political refugees, and economic migrants from poorer countries, including in eastern Europe, seeking work. Unemployment and disadvantage among minority groups, including Gypsies and Travellers, continued at high levels and they increasingly organised in protest.

Major's government resisted women's continuing calls for stronger legislation on equal pay and sex discrimination, convinced that regulation hindered the free market. In 1994 the government responded reluctantly to a directive by the EU (as the EEC had recently become) extending rights to maternity leave including to part-timers but refused to introduce paternity leave. Britain had the worst provision for working parents in the EU and trailed in most areas of gender equality. In 1992 women were at last allowed to become full members of the armed forces, due to a shortage of male recruits, but mainly in support and medical, not combat, roles.

In 1994 the homosexual age of consent was lowered to 18, after three teenagers, backed by the gay rights organization, Stonewall, brought a successful case to the European Court of Human Rights, but the government refused to lower it to 16 to match the heterosexual age. There were unsuccessful protests about the long-established ban on homosexuals in the armed services. It was lifted in 2000 following a ruling in the European Court of Justice, the Supreme Court of the EU established to rule on matters concerning EU law.

Discrimination against older people had long existed and been taken for granted, but resistance gradually grew. In all higher income countries life expectancy was rising while birth-rates fell. The proportion of people over 65 in the UK rose to an unprecedented 15.7% in 1990. There was international panic about declining populations of working age having to fund the needs of growing numbers of older people, stereotyped as frail, dependent and past work. In fact, more people, including in Britain, remained healthy later in life, especially better-off White people. Older people increasingly resisted having to retire at a fixed age and being thought unsuitable, even in their forties and fifties, for promotion or further training, including in modern technology, contrary to much evidence. More wanted to stay longer in work because they felt fit and active and because Conservative policies had eroded the value of state and many occupational pensions. The Campaign against Age Discrimination in Employment formed in 1988 was active through the 1990s, with little effect. In 1990 the European Court of Justice upheld a claim by a man that the lower state pension age of 60 for women (established in 1940) was a (most unusual) case of discrimination against men. In response, the government announced a gradual rise in the female pension age to 65 from 2010 to 2020, though it failed to fully inform women of this.

The defence budget was cut more severely than at any time since 1945, while the armed forces were increasingly active. Nuclear weapons were eliminated, apart from the submarine-based Trident missile which entered service in 1994. Major was determined that the UK should remain influential in the UN, as the smallest member of the five-nation Security Council. In early 1991 service men and women were engaged in 'Desert Storm', the UN mission to liberate Kuwait from invasion by Iraq. In 1992 the UK joined the UN intervention in the post-communist civil war in the Balkans.

Major was not involved in crises in the Commonwealth where racial tension intensified in South Africa until the White President, F.W. de Clerk, sought compromise. Nelson Mandela, early leader of the campaign for racial equality, was released from prison in 1991 after 27 years and he and de Clerk negotiated the end of apartheid. In 1994 South Africa held its first democratic, multiracial election and Mandela became President, within the Commonwealth. Hong Kong was preparing to be handed over to Chinese control in 1997, but most of the arrangements had been negotiated between Thatcher and the Chinese government and the handover came after Major lost the 1997 election to Labour. However, in 1994 he appointed the former Conservative MP, Chris Patten, as the last British governor of Hong Kong. Patten created immediate and lasting tension with China by making Hong Kong's Legislative Council fully democratically elected for the first time, as it had not been through its long history of British rule, and as China did not intend.

Major announced his support for close involvement in the EEC and for the inclusion of former Communist states, but he was critical of its growing powers, though less stridently than Thatcher. When the Maastricht Treaty of European Union was agreed in 1991/92, Britain opted out of the new common currency (the euro) and the Social Chapter which introduced employment standards, including a minimum wage, to be implemented throughout what was from 1993 the European Union (EU).[27] These were anathema to neoliberals whom he was anxious to keep onside. Labour increasingly supported the EU as a bulwark against neoliberalism.

Major had to call an election in 1992, with unemployment close to three million and a flagging economy. He adopted a 'man of the people' image, speaking in the streets, on a (fabricated) soap box, of creating a 'classless society', appealing to voters who had bought their council houses and shares in privatised companies, attacking the "Socialists'" promises to raise taxes and improve services as reprehensible 'tax and spend' policies.[28] He won a clear but reduced majority in April 1992. Kinnock resigned as Labour leader and former Minister, Scottish John Smith, was elected to succeed him.

Major had supported Britain joining the ERM in 1990 but it joined at too high an exchange rate against the US dollar. The resulting pressure on the pound led to large sales of sterling on international markets by 16 September 1992, 'Black Wednesday' as it became known. The Bank of England responded by making the largest sale of its reserves in history, interest rates rose, and Britain left the ERM that evening in an atmosphere of serious crisis. The pound was devalued by 10%. Cuts to public spending followed and tax increases, hitting the low-paid hardest. Interest rates and inflation fell and the economy recovered by 1994, but the government never recovered from what were seen as its misjudgements leading to Black Wednesday.[29] It deepened Europhobia in the Conservative party. Labour established a lasting lead in the opinion polls.

Over the next two years the government's reputation sank further as a succession of ministers were revealed to have been involved in illicit sexual and financial affairs. In response Major appealed to the nation to 'Get Back to Basics' and unite behind 'common sense British values'. Echoing Thatcher, he pledged to promote 'accepting responsibility for yourself and your family and not shuffling it off on the state...', attacking dubious financial transactions and 'permissiveness' in sexual relations, without revealing that in the 1980s he had an adulterous affair with a parliamentary colleague Edwina Currie. This only became public in 2002. But transgressions continued. In the next months one minister was revealed to have fathered an illegitimate child, two to have had secret gay relationships, among other sexual scandals.[30] Then two junior ministers resigned when it was revealed that they had accepted bribes from the Middle Eastern owner of Harrods department store to ask parliamentary questions on his behalf. And another junior minister, Jonathan Aitken, was accused of allowing the Saudi royal family to pay his hotel expenses when he was on official business negotiating an arms deal with the Saudi Arabian government. In 1999 he was imprisoned for lying about the transaction in court.[31]

Major was weakened further in a divided party. He was caught on tape referring to 'three bastards' among his Ministers, assumed to be arch-Thatcherites Michael Portillo, Peter Lilley and John Redwood. He sank in the polls, despite introducing the National Lottery in 1994 which proved a popular way of raising funds to replace public spending mainly on the arts and national heritage, run by a private company. Plans to privatise Royal Mail were shelved in 1994 due to backbench and popular opposition, but sales of rail services, also unpopular, were rushed through. In 1995 Major announced he would stand for re-election as party leader, to make his critics 'put up or shut up'. He easily defeated Thatcherite John Redwood but remained weakened and isolated.[32]

Then in 1996 came a different crisis. Bovine Spongiform Encephalopathy (BSE), known as 'mad cow' disease, had killed millions of cattle when it emerged that it could transmit a severe degenerative disease to humans, Creuzfeldt-Jacob Disease (CJD). There was panic over the numbers expected to die - about 117 people died from CJD in Britain over the next twenty-five years. The panic reduced beef consumption and there was an international ban on British beef, including in the EU, which hurt farmers and did Major little good. The origin of the crisis was deregulation in the 1980s of procedures for feeding and slaughtering animals. Stricter regulation was reintroduced.

Bombing and deaths continued in Northern Ireland and in Britain. Ninety-nine people were injured and three killed across England in 1992. More followed alongside unsuccessful attempts by Major and the Irish government to negotiate a settlement with both sides. In 1996 a bomb at the newly developed Docklands financial centre in London, Canary Wharf, killed two people, injured 100 and caused £100m damage. In Northern Ireland 333 people were killed in 1996.[33]

Labour under John Smith prepared to reshape itself, including agreeing a more democratic constitution which reduced the power of trade unions in conference decisions. Women were increasingly active in the party and in 1993, to overcome discrimination against women entering parliament, persuaded Smith and the party conference to agree all-women shortlists (AWS) in parliamentary candidate selections in half of all vacant Labour-held seats and half of all other seats deemed winnable. In 1996 this was successfully challenged in court by disappointed men as sex discrimination, though it came too late to affect selections for the 1997 election. Smith (aged 55) died suddenly from a heart attack in May 1994 and the choice of successor was between the Shadow Chancellor, Gordon Brown, and Shadow Home Secretary, Tony Blair, both in their forties. They agreed, on terms that remain unclear, that Blair would stand, and he won a majority of the party electorate against trade unionist John Prescott who became deputy leader. Blair called for a 'modern', later called 'New Labour', agenda, rejecting both neoliberalism and what he represented as the traditional views of 'Old Labour', seeking to unite the party while promoting the aspirations of 'Middle England' as the middle-class expanded and the traditional working-class dwindled. He worked hard at media presentation and party membership rose.[34]

The election came on 1 May 1997. Unemployment was close to two million, the economy was not flourishing, middle-class people suffered from rising prices, public sector workers from pay restraints and cuts to services, which were widely unpopular, and the Conservatives from scandals, all of which benefited Labour, whose leaders emphasised their moderation. It achieved the biggest swing against the Conservatives since 1945 and an overall majority of 179. But the turnout (71.5%[35]) was the lowest since 1935 and especially low in some of Labour's traditional heartlands, where unemployment was high. Blair's appeal to Middle England made working-class voters feel neglected, though Blair was MP for Sedgefield in north-east England, a constituency suffering from the decline of coalmining. The Conservatives won their smallest number of seats since 1906 (165) and none in Scotland or Wales. An unprecedented 120 female MPs were elected (out of 659), 102 Labour following All Women Shortlists, thirteen Conservatives, three Liberal Democrats. There were five women in Blair's first Cabinet (out of twenty-three) more than ever before. An unprecedented nine Black and Asian MPs were elected. Major resigned as party leader and was succeeded by William Hague, one of four successive leaders 1997-2005 (Hague, Ian Duncan Smith, Michael Howard, David Cameron) as the party struggled to win support.

1997-2010, 'New Labour'

The new government made no extravagant promises. Blair's popularity grew as he led the extensive public mourning in August 1997 for the death of the 'People's Princess', as he called Princess Diana, estranged wife of the heir to the throne, Prince Charles. Policy developed cautiously. Brown, as Chancellor of the Exchequer, 'prudently' (a favourite word) committed to observing the promise of his Conservative predecessor to limit public spending and avoid tax rises through 1997-1999. But he made significant changes designed to revive the economy. He unexpectedly transferred management of interest rates from the Treasury to the Bank of England and established the Financial Services Authority (FSA) to control financial institutions excessively deregulated by the Conservative government. Prudence enabled him to pay off the inherited deficit by

1998. He promised not to raise direct taxes, but raised indirect taxes on consumption, including fuel tax, presented as protecting the environment (a Labour commitment) as well as raising revenue. It caused protests by lorry drivers and others. Overseas aid (another Labour commitment) grew by 25% in 1999. Also, in 1999 Labour raised arts funding and later abolished admission charges for museums introduced by Thatcher.

Nationalist demands for independent powers continued in Scotland and Wales. Scotsman John Smith had committed Labour to devolution, i.e., transfer of certain powers from Westminster to elected assemblies in both countries. In referenda in September 1997 Scotland voted 74.3% for devolution, Wales 50.3% on a 50% turnout for a devolved assembly with fewer powers than that in Scotland. The Scottish Parliament, as they chose to call it, had quite extensive domestic powers including limited authority to levy taxes, but the UK Parliament retained key areas including social security, economic and monetary policy, the labour market, energy, defence and foreign affairs. The Welsh Assembly had more limited powers and none to raise taxes. The first elections were held in May 1999 under the Additional Member Proportional Representation (PR) system. Women campaigned in both countries for PR, which benefited women candidates internationally. Labour rejected proposals to introduce PR for Westminster elections, fearing it would lose seats. In both countries Labour and the Nationalist parties and in Scotland the Liberal Democrats put up equal numbers of male and female candidates. 41.7% of representatives in the first Welsh Assembly were female. In Scotland 37.2% of the first MSPs were female, compared with 18.2% of MPs in Westminster. The second election in 2002 returned 51.7% females in Wales, the first elected assembly in the world with a female majority.

In both countries female representatives pressed successfully for more progressive social policies than in England.[36] The first and second Scottish governments were Labour/Liberal Democrat coalitions, the third from 2007 a minority Scottish National Party (SNP) government, from 2011 a majority government until 2021 when it formed a coalition with the Greens. Labour governed in Wales throughout, usually in a minority.

Labour also reformed the Westminster parliament. It aimed to end the voting rights of hereditary peers, but the most the Lords would accept was retaining ninety-two voters, elected by their 759 fellow hereditaries. Blair created 380 life peers, more than any previous premier, bringing the total to 603 by 2008.[37] No party had a majority in the Lords, which defeated the government 365 times 1997-2005, though by no means always resisting progress. In 2005 it lost its ancient role as the highest court of appeal, replaced from 2009 by a Supreme Court consisting of high-ranking judges who were not automatically members of the House of Lords. The Commons' timetable was brought closer to a normal working week, including ending all-night sittings. From 2000, party spending in elections and donations to parties were restricted. From 2006 the age of eligibility to stand for parliament or other public office was reduced to 18 to match the voting age.

Labour promised in its election manifesto to restore elected government to Greater London. It proposed a Greater London Authority (GLA) with more limited powers than the previous GLC, with a directly elected mayor and an elected Assembly with powers to hold the mayor to account. The mayor would oversee Transport for London, including setting fares and the use of roads, fund house building and promote economic, social and environmental development. This was accepted by a referendum in Greater London in 1998. In 2000 both the mayor and Assembly were elected by PR. The previous GLC mayor Ken Livingstone was re-elected, but as an Independent because Blair and Brown rejected him as excessively Old Labour. He used his limited powers with moderation and was allowed to stand for Labour in future elections. He introduced the UK's first congestion charge, limiting traffic and pollution in central London by charging vehicles for entry during working hours. He improved public transport and reduced fares.

Blair proposed similar devolution for other regions of England. In 2004 this was put to a referendum in North-East England, for a region of 2.7 million people centred upon Newcastle-upon-Tyne. It was so decisively rejected, by 78% to 22% on a 41.7% turnout, that plans for similar referenda elsewhere were abandoned. Under the Local Government Act, 2000, local authorities could opt for leadership by an elected mayor. It was not obligatory, though the government encouraged large authorities to elect mayors (there were 15 by 2015) and promised revival of local authority powers. But close central control continued and the government did not significantly increase local funding.

Labour extended citizens' rights. The Data Protection Act, 1998, allowed individuals to access their personal data in official records and protect it from disclosure to unauthorised people. The Freedom of Information Act, 2000, allowed requests to all public authorities for previously restricted information. Journalists especially relished it. The Human Rights Act, 1998, embedded the European Convention on Human Rights (established in 1950) in UK law, requiring public authorities to observe the Convention. One outcome was the Equality and Human Rights Commission (EHRC) established in 2007, which took over existing legal responsibilities for gender, race and disability equalities and extended them to include gay, transgender and age-related rights.

Blair aimed to achieve a negotiated settlement in Northern Ireland. He appointed a woman, Mo Mowlam, as Northern Ireland Secretary, who proved popular and skilful at negotiating with the conflicting groups. She set up all-party talks, conditional on ceasefires, though bombings and deaths continued, mostly due to an intransigent group, the Continuity IRA. The talks were supported by the Irish government and US President Bill Clinton, since the US, home to generations of Irish immigrants, felt committed to Irish interests. Blair and Clinton were on good terms. The outcome was the Belfast/Good Friday Agreement, signed in 1998 by all those closely involved. It proposed an administration in which the opposing sides shared executive power and an Assembly elected by PR, to be ratified by referenda north and south of the border. It was praised by Mandela and other international leaders. In referenda in May 1998 North and South voted in favour of the agreement. In June elections the protestant Ulster Unionist Party (UUP) narrowly won most votes but refused to take power until there was lasting peace. Killings by dissident groups continued, despite condemnation from all sides. Fifty-five people died in 1998. Blair worked hard for reconciliation, which was gradually achieved, and the power-sharing executive was functioning by November 1999, with devolved powers. Tensions remained but severe violence ended for the first time in thirty years. It was a major achievement for Blair and Mowlam.[38]

It contributed to Blair's desire to be a major figure in world politics, based on humanitarian 'liberal interventionism' against oppression, he claimed, in close alliance with the US.[39] His first opportunity came in

Kosovo, a mainly Muslim province of the former Yugoslavia which since the fall of Communism had faced aggression from neighbouring Serbia. Blair and Clinton persuaded NATO to intervene in 1999 and the Serbs were defeated.[40] In 2000 Britain launched a limited, successful military operation in the former colony of Sierra Leone to support an elected government against rebellion; then provided aid to assist recovery.

Blair planned to hold a general election in May 2001 but it was delayed by a major epidemic of foot-and-mouth-disease among cattle, the first serious outbreak since 1967. Blair acted quickly to stop movement of cattle to limit spread of the disease and forbade walking in rural areas for the same reason. Some, including the *Guardian,* praised him for 'taking control', Conservatives criticised his 'mishandling', including John Major, no doubt recalling his own difficulties with CJD. Others complained that his measures were too severe, including walkers deprived of their 'right to roam' in the countryside. About six million cattle were slaughtered. Blair pointed out that this was similar to the number killed each year for food, demonstrating the extent of farmers' losses. They received reasonable compensation. By June the epidemic appeared under control and the election was held. Labour won six fewer seats than in 1997, retaining an overwhelming majority of 166, but the turnout was only 59.4%, the lowest since 1918, suggesting declining public support.[41]

Then came the devastating attack on the World Trade Centre in New York on 11 September 2001 (9/11 as it became known), by the militant fundamentalist Muslim Group, Al Qaeda. Suicidal terrorists crashed planes into the buildings, killing 2,977 people. The US President, now Republican George Bush Jnr, son of the previous President Bush, declared war on Afghanistan where Al Qaeda was based, supported by Britain amid widespread revulsion at 9/11. Then in 2003 Bush attacked Iraq, which had no known involvement in 9/11, asserting that it had nuclear 'weapons of mass destruction' and its leader Saddam Hussein threatened world peace.[42] Blair agreed and supported him, though evidence was lacking. The war was strongly opposed in the UK, expressed by an exceptionally large demonstration in London of at least two million people. 139 Labour MPs voted against the war, the largest rebellion against a party whip since the Corn Laws in 1846. Four Ministers who had not been consulted resigned, including Robin Cook, Foreign Secretary 1997-2001 and Leader of the House of Commons at the time of his resignation. Labour party membership fell to the lowest level since its foundation. As the war and that in Afghanistan dragged on with no resolution in sight, Blair's poll ratings plummeted, and Labour crashed in local and European elections in 2004. Then, on 7 July 2005 (later referred to as 7/7) five British Muslim suicide bombers exploded bombs on London transport, killing fifty-two people and injuring over 700, intensifying racism in Britain.

Blair aimed to play a leading role in the EU while remaining close to the US and to strengthen relations between the two. He was not wholly successful, but the UK became a less awkward member than under the Conservatives and he carried some weight.[43] Labour committed to the Social Chapter which set employment standards, part of the Maastricht Treaty agreed in 1991/92, adopting it in 1999 to introduce the UK's first minimum wage, though it was low. Business leaders forecast catastrophic effects, which did not occur. It brought other improvements in workers' rights, especially benefiting women. Part-timers (mostly female) gained equal rights with full-time workers, including to holiday and sickness pay; paid maternity leave was extended and two weeks unpaid paternity leave introduced; women gained the right to return to their previous work or an equivalent after maternity leave and could not be dismissed for any reason connected with maternity or pregnancy; parents could request flexible working hours to match their childcare responsibilities, though employers could refuse; all workers gained greater protection against unfair dismissal and four weeks annual paid leave; night working was restricted; discrimination at work on grounds of gender, age, race, disability, sexual orientation, union membership or part-time working was prohibited; processes for trade union recognition in the workplace were strengthened. Thatcher's restrictions on unions were slightly modified but union membership declined further to 16% of the workforce by 2006, surviving mainly in the public sector.[44]

Blair supported free movement throughout the EU and the inclusion of former communist countries, expanding the EU from fifteen to twenty-five nations in 2004. He also favoured joining the euro, but Brown strongly opposed UK interest rates being set in Europe and, with the UK economy now outperforming most of the eurozone, saw no economic case for entry. Europhobia persisted. The anti-EU UK Independence Party (UKIP) was founded in 1993 in opposition to the Maastricht Treaty. With the slogan 'Take Back Control of our Country' it gained support from opponents of free movement, especially as the EU expanded to include low-income east Europeans who were accused of migrating to take work and welfare from British citizens. But it gained few votes, especially outside England, and no seats in national or local elections.

Brown took much of the responsibility for social policy. In 1999 he introduced the Working Families' Tax Credit (WFTC), a means-tested supplement through the tax system for the low paid. It helped reduce poverty but, as always with means-testing, about 500,000 eligible workers failed to apply, and it encouraged continuing low pay. Inflation was low and unemployment fell to under 1m in 2001. Reducing unemployment was a Labour commitment. 'Work is the best welfare' had been a Labour argument from its foundation. The party believed in providing positive assistance to find work rather than 'incentivising' it by punitive withdrawal of benefits like their Conservative predecessors and successors. Brown imposed a £5bn 'windfall tax' on the privatised utilities, including gas and electricity; it was spent on advice and training for unemployed 18-25 year-olds, 500,000 of whom found work. Unemployed single mothers were also helped to find work or training, assisted by free childcare as well as advice and benefits.[45] But skill levels and productivity remained low compared with other nations. Blair and Brown aimed to stimulate economic growth and social improvement through co-operation with business and investment in education and training to improve skills.

Means-testing of cash benefits grew but Labour substantially increased funding for universal services including education. Educational Maintenance Allowances (EMAs) were introduced to enable young people from low-income families to stay in education or training to age 18. Funding for education increased in deprived areas, improving outcomes including for ethnic minorities, especially in London, though substantial socio-economic and ethnic gaps in performance remained. To help disadvantaged children, tests were introduced at age five to identify needs, also after-school and school holiday clubs. Guidelines for school meals encouraged healthy eating. To promote equality, children with learning difficulties were moved where feasible from their previous 'special' schools to mainstream schools with support provided. Local authorities continued to lose education powers. To limit public spending the government encouraged the continued shift of state schools to private funding and control. From 2000 schools judged to be failing were required to make this shift and were re-branded as 'Academies', 'to improve pupil performance and break the cycle of low expectation' as Minister for Education David Blunkett put it. Over two hundred schools had converted by 2010. High targets were set for performance at age 11 with national tests, and for schools' performance at GCSE. The secondary curriculum was increasingly controlled, though not in Academies. But there was a shortage of teachers as class sizes fell, despite pay rises. Increased controls and wider alternative opportunities made teaching less attractive. Unqualified teaching assistants were recruited.[46] Many school buildings needed renovation. To restrain public spending further, Brown adopted the Private Finance Initiative (PFI) (originally introduced but little used by Major) for these and other public building works, including in the NHS. Private firms owned and operated the work, leasing the buildings back to the public sector at considerable profit. As critics pointed out, it saved the public purse in the short-term at considerable long-term cost.

Blair's main contribution to higher education was to introduce fees of £1,000 pa and abolish maintenance grants. Costs were growing as student numbers rose, belatedly matching those of other higher income countries, though many European countries did not charge fees. In 1999 Blair promised that by 2010 50% of the population would receive higher education by the age of 30, up from 43% then. It was not quite achieved. Backbench and student opposition to fees led to the introduction of means-tested loans for low-income students, to prevent the socio-economic division growing further, and universities received £40m for hardship funds for those who exhausted their loans. Universities meeting targets for numbers of students from state schools and lower socio-economic classes received 5% additional funding, but the numbers did not rise. Scotland refused to impose fees; Wales had no such powers but did its best to restrain costs to students. From 2006 universities could charge fees of up to £3,000. Following more demonstrations, more generous grants and bursaries were introduced.[47]

The financial sector continued to flourish and pay and bonuses to soar. Blair, who later amassed a considerable fortune, expressed no criticism. He wrote in 2002, 'We favour true equality; equal worth and equal opportunity, not an equality of outcome focused on incomes alone'.[48] He aimed to improve the conditions of the poorest without disadvantaging the rich. Low incomes rose 1997-2007 due to lower unemployment, higher pay and improved benefits, while the top 1% rose fastest. Income inequality continued to grow, though more slowly than since the 1980s.[49] Tax and social security changes under New Labour were more redistributive than any since 1979, though they did not publicise this for fear of disturbing the voters of Middle England. Britain remained one of the most unequal higher income countries, though outstripped by the US.

From 1997-2008 poverty among pensioners fell from 20% to 14% as the value of pensions rose, though they were still inadequate for survival and among the least generous in the higher income world. A more generous means-tested supplement, Pension Credit (PC), was introduced in 1999, along with free travel on public transport, an annual winter fuel payment for all pensioners and free TV licences from age 75. Again a high proportion of eligible people failed to apply for the means-tested PC and poverty remained high, especially among women (the majority of over-65s since women on average lived longer) and ethnic minorities. Other older people were wealthy, benefiting from large private pensions and the value of their homes as prices continued to rise. This gave rise to assertions about the wealth of the whole 'baby boomer' generation which they were said to lavish on selfish personal pleasure while younger people suffered relative deprivation.[50] In reality many wealthy older people gave substantial support to their children and grandchildren in their lifetimes as well as contributing a great deal to the wider community, while many others, as we have seen, lived in poverty. Socio-economic inequalities were growing in all age groups and were as great within as between generations.[51] Benefits for disabled people improved.

In 1999 Blair pledged to end child poverty by 2020. Lower unemployment, support for single mothers to find work, increased Child Benefit and Tax Credits helped reduce it by 1.1m by 2010, from about 28% to 17% of children in Great Britain.[52] In 1998 Brown announced a 'Sure Start' programme for children under 4, initially in deprived areas, then spreading widely as it became popular and successful, providing childcare, health care, early learning and support and advice to parents, designed to improve children's life chances from their earliest years.

Funding for housing grew very little, despite the acute shortage of low-cost homes which contributed to poverty. More 'social' housing was transferred to housing associations, and local authorities could require private developers to provide a proportion of 'affordable' housing in each new development, though few did so. Housebuilding fell to one of its lowest points since 1947. In 2000 just 22,000 publicly owned homes were completed, a typical year. House prices and private rents rose, and the numbers of homeless people continued to grow. Hostel accommodation was provided, but housing was one of New Labour's biggest failures.[53]

The NHS fared better. Funding rose from £30bn to £90bn 1997-2007, reaching the EU average. More went to deprived areas. There were serious efforts to improve services and equalise them across the country. Targets were introduced which reduced long waiting times for diagnosis or treatment. Treatment of heart conditions and cancer care improved, after falling behind international standards. NHS Direct was introduced in 1998, a 24-hour telephone advice and information service for England, staffed by trained nurses. Corresponding services developed in Wales and Scotland. NHS walk-in clinics opened. The National Institute for Clinical Excellence (NICE) was founded in 1999 to improve and equalise standards of health services across England and Wales, assisted in England by Primary Care Groups, from 2001 named Primary Care Trusts (PCTs), established across the country to commission primary health care and provide community public health services. From 2002 they were guided by the priorities of Strategic Health Authorities which were established to create a coherent framework for the development of services across the full range of NHS institutions in all localities, with uneven outcomes. Similar arrangements were introduced in Wales and Scotland. There was a continuous process of adaptation of the management of the complex range of publicly funded health services, aiming to provide better care, more equal in quality and accessible to all in need, reversing the cuts and privatisation since 1979.

Hospitals became 'Foundation Trusts', managing their own budgets and services, competing to provide services in an 'internal market'. The resulting costs and quality of hospital management were criticised in parliament, but outcomes and patient satisfaction improved, staffing levels rose by 25%, waiting times fell. Hospitals were cleaner and hospital-acquired infections fell. Medical students increased by 50%, nursing students by 30%, GPs by 9% between 1997 and 2007, though 66% of the most deprived areas still had fewer GPs in 2005 than the average. Prevention was emphasised as a national public health strategy. Smoking was banned in enclosed public spaces, with remarkably little resistance, in Scotland in 2006, England, Wales and Northern Ireland in 2007. Abortion services improved despite persistent opposition. Health, including hospital, services remained imperfect, but their quality and integration were much improved.[54]

Obesity was a growing cause of ill-health, encouraged by the increasing availability and popularity of cheap fast foods. Rising demand for healthcare was also due to the continuing rise in life expectancy, though to a lesser extent than often believed because more people remained healthy later in life. By 2010 a record 16% of the UK population were aged 65 and over, but still there were substantial socio-economic inequalities: in London, males born in wealthy Kensington could expect to live for an average 88 years, in poorer, mixed-race Tottenham 71 years, alongside a range of variations in length of life and of healthy life among women and men across London and Britain.[55]

As more people lived longer more worked longer, because they wanted to or needed the income, though, especially if they became unemployed, older people still faced discrimination in the labour market. The government encouraged later retirement to cut state pension costs and in 2007 proposed gradually raising the state pension age to 68 from 2044-2046, far enough ahead to stem protest. The TUC pointed out that

20% of workers, generally the lower-paid, already retired before 65 due to ill-health. From 2001 the birth-rate unexpectedly rose, after declining since the late 1960s, potentially countering fears of the costs of an ageing society, assisted by immigration of mainly younger workers, though neither gain was widely recognised. Healthy older people made substantial contributions to the community. Those aged 65-74 were the most active age group in the voluntary sector and many grandparents helped their families with childcare. The University of the Third Age, founded in 1982, provided opportunities for older people to get together to enjoy continued learning, as thousands did across the UK. They also continued to expose and resist discrimination, including in 1998 founding the Third Age Employment Network (TAEN) to advise on and encourage work and training for older people. In 2000 the government responded with New Deal 50+ to help over 50s find work: 120,000 succeeded by 2004. Also, in 2000 an EU Directive on Equal Treatment in Employment specified age as a dimension of inequality for the first time. The UK gradually, partially, implemented it: from 2006 workers could request to work past fixed retirement ages, but employers could refuse. Following protest, Labour abolished fixed retirement ages except where employers could demonstrate that workers could no longer work efficiently, implemented in 2011 after Labour lost office. But discrimination continued. In 2011 a woman successfully brought a case for age and sex discrimination against the BBC when she was sacked as a TV presenter, aged 53, on grounds of age, while her visibly older male co-presenter continued. Age discrimination in healthcare was another long-standing issue against which there was growing protest. For example, women were regularly called for screening for breast cancer only to age 70, though it was more common in women over 70. In 2005 a national survey found more people reporting discrimination on grounds of age (29%) than any other cause. When the EHRC was established in 2007 age discrimination was part of its brief.[56]

The BBC case was just one of many examples of women protesting against inequality, with good reason. They outperformed males at all levels of education and more were employed, but still concentrated in low-paid, low status work with few in top jobs. The average gender pay gap was 27.5% in 1997, 16.4% in 2010. Following the male legal challenge to All Women Shortlists, Labour shifted to 50/50 male/female shortlists. Six fewer female Labour MPs were elected in 2001. Then the Sexual Discrimination (Election Candidates) Act, 2002, freed all parties to take positive action to extend female representation. Labour revived AWS but there was little obvious action by other parties. The 2005 election returned 128 women (including ninety-eight Labour, seventeen Conservative), a record 20% of MPs. John Smith's promise to follow the EU policy of 'gender mainstreaming', integrating gender equality within all policies and programmes, received only token implementation.[57]

Similarly, gay protest continued, and inequalities gradually narrowed. In 1997 the first MPs came out publicly: two males, one female, all Labour. In 1998 the age of sexual consent was equalised with that of heterosexuals at 16, following a successful appeal to the European Court of Human Rights. In 1999 the ban on lesbian, gay and transgender people serving in the armed forces was lifted, also following an ECHR ruling. In 2000 Scotland repealed Section 28 of the Local Government Act, 1988, which, as previously discussed, prohibited local authorities from taking measures to counter homophobia, including schools incorporating respect for gay people in sex education classes. This was followed in 2003 in England, Wales and Northern Ireland. In 2004 the Civil Partnership Act granted same sex couples the same rights as married heterosexual couples. In 2006 discrimination in provision of goods and services was outlawed, followed in 2008 by incitement to homophobia. Polls indicated high levels of support for the reforms. Transgender people also increasingly campaigned. In 2002 the ECHR found the UK in breach of their right to marry and receive respect for their private lives. In 2004 they gained the legal right to live in their acquired gender if this had medical support, but discrimination continued.[58]

Continuing poor skill levels was one reason why the government welcomed immigrants from the EU and elsewhere, as the Conservatives had begun, discreetly, to do. Labour eased controls further for the highly skilled and much-needed low-wage workers in hospitality and agricultural work, and for overseas university students, who were allowed to work while studying. Some low-paid migrants were severely exploited. Immigration, legal and illegal, greatly increased, including refugees from crisis-hit Kosovo, Sierra Leone, then Iraq. But it was hard for refugees to enter Britain legally and Labour tightened the restrictions, especially following the 2005 bombings. They received very limited government support and were forbidden to work to support themselves and their families for at least six months after arrival, though they received much help from voluntary, including religious, organisations. They faced hostile accusations of coming to Britain just to gain health and welfare benefits and putting pressure on already over-stretched education, health and housing services, though immigrants who could work contributed more through work and taxes than they took in benefits and services.[59]

Hostility to immigrants increased racial tensions. In 1997 Labour at last set up an inquiry into the death of Stephen Lawrence in 1993, following a campaign by his parents. Chaired by a former High Court judge, Sir William Macpherson, it reported in 1999 with a damning indictment of 'institutional racism' among the police, who had failed to investigate the death properly. The Race Relations (Amendment) Act, 2000, placed an enforceable duty on public authorities, including the police, to promote equal opportunities and eliminate racism. More police were recruited from minorities, some of whom experienced racism at work.[60] The UK population of immigrant origin was increasingly diverse, but continued to suffer disadvantage, including in education, health and employment. Conflicts erupted. In May 2001 in Oldham, Lancashire, hundreds of young Pakistani and Bangladeshi men rioted for three nights and 86 policemen were injured, followed by violence elsewhere, provoked by unemployment and police treatment of young men of colour. The government attempted to increase cohesion and equalise opportunities, while also extending police powers to control crime. Complaints grew of even greater use of stop and search powers against Black and Asian men. Following the 9/11 and 7/7 bombings anti-Muslim attacks and discrimination grew. The number of Black and Asian MPs crept up: twelve in 2001, all Labour, and Paul Boateng became the first Black Cabinet Minister, as Chief Secretary to the Treasury. In 2005 thirteen were elected for Labour and two Conservatives.[61]

Labour survived the general election in 2005 mainly due to the weakness of the Conservatives. It won fewer seats but still had a large majority of 65 after a low turnout (61.4%) especially in working-class constituencies and among opponents of the Iraq war. By 2007, 51% of poll respondents thought Blair 'out of touch with ordinary people'. His determined efforts at positive self-representation in the media ceased to help. In June 2007 he resigned and was replaced by Brown, apparently as agreed when Blair became leader. There was no clear opposition in the party. Before resigning, Blair rushed through measures designed to secure his 'legacy', including expansion of academy schools and renewal of Trident, both much opposed on the Labour backbenches. They passed with Conservative votes.

Brown faced a series of crises. Within three days of his appointment Islamist attacks in London and Glasgow led to the death of a terrorist in Glasgow. There were major floods, then another epidemic of foot-and-mouth disease among cattle. This was dealt with swiftly and well, minimising animal deaths, with lessons learned from the 2001 outbreak. Brown was judged to have handled these crises well and was ahead in the polls. Then in September 2007 a serious financial crisis emerged in the US, where banks had granted too many insecure mortgages. Confidence collapsed internationally and there was a run on banks. The government guaranteed all bank and building society savings up to £35,000, later £85,000, and nationalised the worst hit bank, Northern Rock, to prevent its collapse. But by autumn 2008, after US bank collapses, British bank shares plummeted, and other European countries were hit. The Treasury devised a £500bn international bank rescue plan which Brown persuaded EU and G7 finance ministers to accept. In Britain it required costly part-nationalisation of three big, failing banks: Royal Bank of Scotland, Halifax and Lloyds. In 2009 the Bank of England cut interest rates to an unprecedented 0.5% and printed £75bn of money (known as 'quantitative easing') to subsidise the banks. The Chancellor, Alastair Darling, raised the top rate of income tax from 40% to 45%.

Brown again took the lead internationally, persuading the leaders of the world's twenty leading economies (the G20) to pledge £1.1trillion to the IMF to prevent another collapse. This succeeded but the British economy was hit hard. It was exceptionally dependent upon financial services for employment and tax revenue and many households were in debt. Unemployment rose past 2m in early 2009, retailers suffered from low demand, and some collapsed. Brown was unfairly blamed by the Conservatives for a crisis that had originated in the US and got little credit for averting a worse international crisis. Then the *Daily Telegraph* discovered that some MPs, in all parties, were profiting from dubious expenses claims, including for such essentials as dog food and equipping a pond with a floating duck island. Some were eventually jailed. Brown had a Parliamentary Standards Authority established to prevent such practices, but Labour lost support as the crises continued. It lost control of the Scottish Assembly to the SNP and overall control of the Welsh Assembly. In 2008 Livingstone lost the London mayoral election to the Conservative journalist, Boris Johnson.[62]

A general election was unavoidable in 2010. Brown was tired, preoccupied with the financial crisis, and ran a poor campaign, not helped by Labour having much less funding than the Conservatives. They continued to blame Labour for the crisis while encouraging voters' concerns about immigration, crime and EU membership, assisted by the majority right-wing press. Labour received little credit for its real achieve-ments. But there was not great enthusiasm for the Conservatives. After losing the 2005 election they had again changed their leader for the relatively inexperienced David Cameron, who promoted a moderate 'compassionate Conservatism'. They won but without an overall majority since the Liberal Democrats won fifty-seven seats. They agreed a coalition with the Liberal Democrats, who resisted Labour overtures. There was markedly low support for the Conservatives in the devolved nations: in Scotland they won just one seat, as in 2001 and 2005, Labour won forty-one; in Wales Conservatives won eight, Labour twenty-six. Brown resigned as party leader and in September Ed Miliband was elected his successor. He was moderately left-of-centre, Minister for Energy and Climate Change in Brown's government, with little experience of leadership.

2010-2020

The Coalition government continued until the next election in 2015. It was controlled by the Conservatives who were determined, as clearly expressed by Cameron and the Chancellor George Osborne, to return neoliberalism to the centre of government practice, establishing a regime they called 'Austerity', with low taxes and a small state. Cameron claimed this was essential to repair a Britain 'broken' by Labour's supposed irresponsible spending. He proclaimed a desire to improve social conditions, but not through state welfare: rather a 'Big Society' must replace the 'Big State'. He appeared to mean that voluntary action had been destroyed by state welfare and must be revived to replace it. In fact, it had been very active continuously in the post-war welfare state, increasingly as it strove to maintain services cut by Conservatives. It was an important feature of UK culture.[63] Cameron soon went silent on the issue.

Severe cuts to public services were announced one month after the election, in the June 2010 Budget. More came in the five-year plan of October 2010, which also cut grants to voluntary organisations. It was described by the respected, independent Institute for Fiscal Studies (IFS) as 'the longest, deepest, period of cuts to public services since at least the Second World War'.[64] Privatisation revived. Public sector pay was frozen, Whitehall costs cut by one-third, local authority funding by 30%, Sure Start Centres, social care, youth and other services contracted. Overwhelmingly privatised, childcare services in England became scarcer and more expensive than in any comparable country. In Scotland they were run by local authorities, were much cheaper, with better trained staff. EMA was abolished (not in devolved Scotland and Wales), Child Benefit frozen, and other benefits reduced in value, except those of pensioners, who had voted substantially for the Conservatives and were guaranteed an increase of at least 2.5% p.a. Less predictable younger voters faced the rise in the state pension age to 66 planned by Labour for 2026, brought forward to 2020, along with the planned equalisation of women's pension age. Women were not informed in time to enable preparation and formed the Women Against State Pension Inequality (WASPI) protest group, but it failed to achieve change. Further changes in 2014 brought forward the rise in pension age to 67 for men and women to 2026-2028 and ordained a review of the pension age at least every five years.

The government aimed to eliminate local authority education, reducing its funding and planning to convert all remaining state schools to Academies. 66% were converted by 2015, without evident improvement in standards. Local authorities running successful schools opposed further conversion, supported by parents. State-funded 'free schools' could also now be established, controlled by parents, charities, teachers and others, regardless of local need. Scotland and Wales introduced neither free schools nor Academies, retaining local government control. Government control of the English school curriculum tightened. Universities were allowed, at their discretion, to raise fees to £9,250 a year in England, £9,000 in Wales, as they did gradually in the coming years. Grants and loans were cut. For overseas students fees now averaged £13,500 per year. By 2015 under 20% of university income came from government, but it increased control through regular assessments of teaching and research.

NHS spending rose, much of it on administration, while pay of nursing and allied hospital staff was frozen and demand for services rose. Scotland and Wales sought to protect NHS users by abolishing prescription charges. The Health and Social Care Act, 2012, encouraged outsourcing of English NHS services to the private sector. Public spending on private healthcare rose by £1bn 2014-2019. Staff numbers declined along with conditions, nurses in England from 408,000 in 2008 to 333,000 in 2013; GP numbers also fell. Hospitals fell into deficit and poor care caused a succession of scandals. Waiting lists grew and 'non-essential' operations were reduced and delayed (e.g., for cataract removal or joint replacement) - not life-threatening conditions but seriously hampering many older peoples' independence and increasing their need for other services. But the number and quality of residential and community services for older and disabled people in England and Wales dwindled as local budgets were cut and private providers' profits fell when local authorities could no longer afford to subsidise them or clients to pay higher charges. In Scotland personal care at home or in institutions was free. A government commissioned report chaired by economist Andrew Dilnot in 2011 recommended more government funding and a limit to individual lifetime costs for care. It was welcomed by the government but little changed. From 2010-2016 in England and Wales, 30% fewer people received publicly funded care; growing numbers of older people 'blocked' hospital beds they no longer needed because care they did need was unavailable elsewhere.

The average rise in expected years of life, and of healthy life, slowed from 2011 for the first time in decades, slipping behind most other high-income countries, especially among the poorest and especially among ethnic minorities and women; among women in deprived areas it declined 2013-2018.[65] The birth-rate also began to fall again, after rising since 2001, probably also due to lower incomes and poorer services. Disability benefits were progressively cut, while claimants faced stricter work-capability assessments conducted by private contractors without medical or other relevant skills, designed to force them into work, often inappropriately. Many successful appeals followed which were costly to public funds.

By 2016 only 7% of households lived in council houses, often of poor quality, better housing having been sold. The lack of official concern for council tenants was evident in the Grenfell Tower fire disaster in London in 2017, when seventy-two people died due to poor fire protection and maintenance of a tower block in prosperous, Conservative-controlled, Kensington, despite residents' complaints. The widespread public horror and publicity led the government to establish a public enquiry into the disaster which in early 2023 was still in progress.[66] The government promised funding for removal of unsafe flammable cladding from tall blocks and improved safety measures, but both advanced slowly and controversially. The overall shortage of affordable homes and homelessness continued to grow.

The Coalition and its Conservative successors encouraged the notion still prevalent in the popular media of benefit claimants as irresponsible 'shirkers', defrauding an over-generous system funded by hard-working 'strivers', i.e., taxpayers. Post-war notions of welfare as the right of all citizens in need in a caring society had vanished. On this basis, Universal Credit (UC) was introduced in 2012. A single payment replaced six means-tested benefits: Income Support, Jobseeker's Allowance, Employment and Support Allowance, Housing Benefit, Child Tax Credit and Working Tax Credit. Its main objective was to force anyone judged capable into work, a return to Poor Law principles a century on. In fact a high and rising proportion of UC claimants were in work, but too insecure and low-paid to avoid poverty. All benefits were capped below average wages at low levels.

It was argued that the previous system was too complex, and a single benefit was simpler and cheaper to administer. A complex system had developed because work, family and personal lives are complex. Previously, if circumstances changed for reasons beyond individual control - unemployment, sickness, accident, rising or falling pay or rent - only the relevant benefit would be reassessed. Now one change required reassessment of the whole package, halting all payments for at least five weeks, often much longer because it was inefficiently administered, neither cheaper nor more efficient than the previous system, causing starvation, rent arrears and debt, increasing already severe poverty. Claims could only be made on-line, though many low-income people lacked access to the internet or expertise in using it. Partners in abusive relationships were especially hard hit because UC payments were made monthly into one household bank account, often giving the abusive partner total control. Previously they were made to the relevant claimant e.g., Child Tax Credit normally to the mother. The Scottish government divided all UC payments between partners and paid fortnightly. In 2014 the high costs of administration caused Osborne as Chancellor to reduce the benefit, pushing more people into poverty. UC was tightened further to allow households with at least two children no further payment for additional children born after 6 April 2017. As a spokesperson for the Department of Work and Pensions put it: 'families on benefits are asked to make the same financial decisions as families supporting themselves solely through work', though most claimants affected were in work and the pregnancy might pre-date an unforeseeable crisis. It had no significant effect on birth-rates but became a major cause of child and family poverty. The Children's Commissioners for Scotland, Wales and Northern Ireland all called for it to be scrapped, without success; doing so lay outside their devolved powers. In 2018 the National Audit Office reported that UC was six years behind the timetable for full roll-out and had cost more to administer than the benefits it replaced. Roll-out was still incomplete in early 2023.

Also in 2018 the UN Special Rapporteur on Human Rights and Extreme Poverty, Philip Alston, made an unprecedented tour of Britain. He reported with horror on the extent of poverty and the contribution of the scheme, 'fast falling into Universal Discredit' as he put it, which was making conditions worse, when, 'Social support should be a route out of poverty'.[67] His excoriating report was dismissed by the Westminster government but welcomed by the Scottish government. Westminster proclaimed its policies a success because official unemployment figures were the lowest since 1975. But, unlike in 1975, workers were increasingly in insecure, low-paid work, keeping their families in poverty, without trade union protection due to union decline. In an effectively unregulated labour market, some employers ignored the minimum wage (re-named the 'living wage' by Osborne, which it was not) and workers' rights to sickness and other benefits, in the so-called 'gig economy', often treating employees as self-employed, or placing them on insecure 'zero hours' contracts with uncertain daily or weekly hours and pay. Independent social surveys showed that up to 60% of the exceptionally large numbers in poverty by 2019 were workers, inadequately paid. About 30% of children in UK were in poverty, which was further increased by rising housing costs.[68] Homelessness continued to grow, and there was unprecedented use of food banks by families who could not afford to eat. Food banks were almost unheard of in Britain before 2010, a significant example of voluntary action responding to a welfare crisis. In 2017/18 the largest national food bank, the Trussell Trust, gave out 1.3m food parcels, and the number rose thereafter. There were hundreds of small, local foodbanks and total provision is unknown.[69] Some Ministers applauded this extensive voluntary action rather than seeking to eliminate the deprivation that made it necessary. In October 2022 Alston's newly appointed successor, Olivier de Schutter, repeated his warning about the disturbing extent of poverty in the UK.[70]

Meanwhile another crisis developed as Conservative hostility to EU membership mounted. When David Cameron became Prime Minister, he had little experience of foreign affairs. He decided, like his predecessors, that to restore the economy Britain's international position must be strengthened, requiring a close relationship with the US, active membership of the EU and good relations with Putin's Russia. Despite "Austerity" he insisted on keeping Trident and building costly aircraft carriers, both planned by Brown, as essential, expensive, symbols of Britain's international status. He formed a good relationship with President Sarkozy of France, and they signed a treaty of defence cooperation. In 2011 the "Arab Spring" of popular protest against oppressive governments suggested hope for democracy in the Middle East, with little effect except in Tunisia, which moved from dictatorship to a presidential democracy with an Assembly and President elected every five years, though the President retained and exerted considerable powers and tensions continued. As the governments in Arab countries hit back, Britain and France agreed an air assault against President Gaddafi's repression of opponents in Libya. They needed US support, but President Barack Obama, elected in 2009, wanted to withdraw from the Middle East. Gaddafi was killed and a long civil war followed in Libya. Then in 2013 the leader of Syria, Bashar al-Assad, was said to have used long-banned chemical weapons against rebels. This went too far for Obama who prepared to intervene. Sarkozy was eager to join him, as was Cameron, but parliament refused due to strong opposition to another Middle East war following failures in Iraq then Libya. This ended Cameron's foreign policy ventures. Britain did not rank high in Obama's concerns and their relationship was poor.

Cameron wanted to focus upon domestic issues, but hostility to the EU grew in the party, encouraged by UKIP. There was growing pressure for a referendum on membership. Within the Coalition, the Liberal

Democrat leader Nick Clegg opposed this. Cameron promised that if the Conservatives won the election due in 2015, he would negotiate a new settlement with the EU and hold a referendum. He wanted completion of the single market - intended to establish free movement of goods, services, capital and people throughout the EU. He also requested less 'intrusion' upon national governments and more democratic accountability from Brussels. EU members were shocked by his referendum pledge.

The Conservatives won the election with a twelve-seat majority, ending the Coalition and forcing Cameron to call the referendum. UKIP held only one seat, that of a Conservative defector, but came third in votes with 12.9%. Miliband had not made a strong impact and resigned. In September 2015 Jeremy Corbyn was elected Labour leader by the party. Corbyn had been an MP since 1983, never a Minister. He was well-known as a left-winger, active in anti-war organisations, dubious about EU membership in a party much divided about it. Labour membership increased substantially following his election, especially among younger people.

Certain he would win, Cameron ignored warnings from officials against a simple majority vote in the referendum, despite the closeness of the two sides in opinion polls. Anxious to hold the party together, he made little effort to defend EU membership and promised a substantial cut to immigration as its opponents demanded. A bitter campaign included much misrepresentation by the 'Brexiteers', as they became known, in their demands to "Take Back Control" which overlooked the fact that Britain had, and had always exercised, complete control over which EU directives they chose to adopt. Their well-funded campaign blamed the size of British contributions to the EU budget and the impact of EU migration for the weaknesses of public services, including the NHS, which really resulted from Conservative cuts. It ignored the positive contributions of European workers, including in the NHS, and the benefit to deprived areas, including South Wales and North-East England, of substantial EU subsidies. 'Remainers' stressed the negative effects of leaving rather than the benefits of staying. UK voters overall rejected the EU with a narrow majority of 51.9% to 48.1% from a turnout of 72.2%, but with clear majorities for 'Remain' in Scotland and Northern Ireland. In England younger and better-educated voters were strongly pro-Remain. Altogether just 37.5% of qualified voters voted to leave. Cameron resigned.

Leading Brexiteers, including the most prominent, Boris Johnson (Mayor of London - which overwhelmingly voted Remain - until 2016, a Conservative MP from 2015), appeared as unprepared for the result as Cameron, who had banned Whitehall from detailed contingency planning. No-one had addressed the complexities separation from the EU, the UK's largest market, would bring, including on the Irish border. Since the Belfast/Good Friday Agreement there had been an open border between the North and the Republic of Ireland, which was in the EU, and frequent movement between the countries. This was likely to become difficult when the North left the EU, hence its strong Remain vote; the issue was to destabilise Northern Ireland government for several years.

Cameron was succeeded by Theresa May, previously Home Secretary, a low profile Remainer with little experience of foreign affairs. She mistrusted civil servants as too uniformly pro-Remain and relied upon a small circle of inexperienced advisers for negotiating the exit from the

EU. She set out 'red lines' designed to make Britain "a fully sovereign, independent nation": no freedom of movement across its borders; British law no longer decided by the European Court of Justice; leaving the single market and customs union but keeping an open border between the North and South of Ireland because it was regularly crossed for trade, work and other purposes and losing it would be very disruptive. But these objectives were wholly incompatible. May refused to discuss them with the devolved UK assemblies or to allow them to participate in discussions with the EU. Boris Johnson, now Foreign Secretary, insisted that Britain could leave the EU and keep all its advantages - 'having its cake and eating it' as critics commented - to the irritation of the Europeans. They were determined not to grant an easy deal. In the EU Britain had traded easily with the rest of the world. Brexiteers argued that the lost EU market would be replaced by deals with the world's most dynamic economies, underestimating how difficult and slow this could be. Over three years of uncertainty before Britain finally left the EU on 31 January 2020 business investment stalled.

Brexiteers believed that a strong relationship with Washington would secure Britain's world influence, but Obama thought leaving the EU made Britain a less useful partner. He built close links with Germany instead. The election of Donald Trump to the US Presidency in 2016 added to the uncertainty. He had no interest in Britain and promoted a nationalist nostalgia, similar to that of the Brexiteers, to "Make America Great Again". They shared hostility to immigrants. Trump feted Nigel Farage, leader of UKIP, and pulled out of international agreements.

May called a sudden election in June 2017, perhaps hoping to boost her status and power in the country and the party since the Conservatives were well ahead in polls. But the poll lead dropped as the campaign progressed. She had miscalculated and lost her overall majority. Labour under Corbyn won more votes, 12.8m, than in any election since 1997 - to the horror of his many opponents in the party who thought him too left-wing - just 789,225 votes but 56 seats behind the Conservatives. UKIP gained no seats, only 1.8% of the votes and declined thereafter. Farage resigned. In April 2019 he founded the Brexit Party, aiming to ensure that Britain left the EU after almost three years' delay. The Conservatives remained weakly in government following a deal with the Eurosceptic Democratic Unionist Party (DUP) of Northern Ireland, which favoured stronger barriers between the Republic and the North, where divisions were reviving.

One week after the election May responded to the Grenfell Tower fire crisis indecisively and with her characteristic lack of empathy and social skills. Then in April 2018 the *Guardian* exposed what became known as the 'Windrush scandal'. As Home Secretary May had developed a policy of seeking out and punishing illegal immigrants, creating what she described as 'a hostile environment'. The *Guardian* revealed that many people who had moved to Britain wholly legally from the Commonwealth, often as young children accompanying their parents, were being punished as illegal migrants if they could not provide documentary evidence of their right to remain in Britain, which until 1973 was the right of anyone born in the Commonwealth. A high proportion of victims had migrated from the Caribbean, and it became known as the 'Windrush scandal' because in 1948 one of the first substantial groups of immigrants from the Caribbean arrived at Southampton aboard HMS Windrush, amid much publicity. Many who had not kept documents confirming their long-ago arrival found that the Home Office also appeared to have no record of their status and they were detained or lost their rights to work, to benefits and health care, driving them into destitution, sometimes death. Some were returned to their country of birth, where they might have no links. As many personal stories of unjust, damaging treatment were revealed, May and the Home Office faced severe criticism. In December 2018 a compensation scheme was established for victims, but redress was very slow.[71] In 2023 many people were still uncompensated and suffering exclusion.

Meanwhile May proposed her compromise EU deal to the Cabinet in July 2018. Leading Brexiteers, Johnson and David Davis, resigned. Leaving Europe, planned for 29 March 2019, was delayed while negotiations continued, amid warfare in the Tory party between supporters of compromise and advocates of a 'clean break'. May failed three times to get a compromise agreement past the Commons. In the election for the EU parliament in May 2019, the Brexit Party gained the largest share of votes with 31.6%, the Conservatives only 9.1% (Labour 14.1%); the turn-out was 37.18%. In June May resigned.

Boris Johnson won the party leadership with an anti-EU campaign, promising to leave with or without a deal. He called an election in December 2019, boasting of Britain's "Return to Greatness". The campaign exposed Labour's divisions. Some leading members called for a second referendum since polls showed widespread doubts about Brexit, while Corbyn prevaricated. The Conservatives triumphed with an 80-seat overall majority, winning a substantial number of traditional Labour seats in Northern England - labelled the 'red wall' - perhaps helped by Johnson's (unfulfilled) promises to 'end austerity'. The Brexit Party stood only in Labour-held seats. Its 44 candidates won no seats and just 2% of votes overall, many more in Brexit supporting Labour constituencies - 30.4% in Barnsley Central, which Labour held. It probably contributed to the Conservative majority. Labour slumped with 203 seats, its worst result since 1935. Corbyn resigned and the centrist Sir Keir Starmer, former Director of Public Prosecutions, politically inexperienced, was elected to replace him. Johnson signed a withdrawal agreement which failed to solve the Irish border problem, and Britain left the EU on 31 January 2020.

Despite the belief of Brexiteers that Britain liberated from the EU would become a major global trading nation, it was isolated with no clear international role in an increasingly unstable world. It kept its seat on the UN Security Council, was the fifth largest economy in the world and belonged to the G7 and G20. The armed forces were strong, its intelligence and diplomatic services internationally highly rated, it had an exceptionally large overseas aid budget and still led the Commonwealth. But the economy was weakening again; by 2022 it was judged to have slipped to the sixth largest economy. It was dependent upon the US for security and lacked a substitute for EU intelligence cooperation, including against the persistent danger of terrorists and cyber-attacks. There was also a real danger of the break-up of the UK deepened by divisions over EU membership, with growing tension in Northern Ireland.

The future became even more uncertain with the unexpected emergence of the Covid-19 pandemic shortly after Brexit. The UK was slower than many other countries to impose restrictions when it started and when it revived in autumn 2020, perhaps because the premier was preoccupied with Brexit and other matters, though he was himself hospitalised with Covid in April 2020. Thereafter his government lacked consistent policies and the devolved governments followed different, often more effective, approaches, further revealing differences across the nations. The first 'lockdown' covered the whole UK from March - June 2020. The UK economy has never in modern history shut down so extensively for so long, with closure of 'non-essential' shops and businesses including restaurants, pubs, flower shops, while supermarkets flourished. This caused high unemployment especially among the lowest paid, further increasing poverty, use of food banks and homelessness. Nor had schools previously closed for so long. Disrupted education exposed stark class differences between richer children with greater access to computers and other devices for distance learning, more space and more parental support for home learning, with potentially harmful effects on the futures of poorer children, including from the loss of free school meals.[72]There were further disruptions when schools and universities temporarily reopened and Covid spiked again, infecting teachers and students. Further lockdowns in 2020 were limited regionally but had serious social and economic effects.

From the start of lockdowns people suffering from health conditions which made them especially vulnerable to infection were required to self-isolate at home. Initially the government ordered everyone over age 70 to do so, until prominent septuagenarians complained that this was age discrimination: they were healthier than many younger people. The government then required isolation based on health not age. Working people expected to self-isolate after contact with Covid victims were eligible for sickness benefits of only £95.95 per week, the lowest in the high-income world. And, as suggested above, at least two million insecure, low-paid workers lacked access to sick pay. Better-paid workers could mostly work from home on full pay. Many on low incomes lacked this option and felt they must go to work, risking sickness and infecting others, to avoid destitution. Despite the difficulties, lockdowns were generally carefully observed - except, it was later revealed, by the Prime Minister who attended parties in Downing St, gatherings that were banned for everyone else. Largely due to widespread condemnation of this thoughtless behaviour he resigned in July 2022, followed by two PMs in quick succession and a period of considerable confusion in government.

Countries which locked down earliest and introduced effective systems to test, trace and isolate carriers of the virus had fewest Covid victims. The UK had very high rates of infection and, a year into the pandemic, one of the highest death rates per head of population in the world, 169 per 100,000 by February 2021. Testing for the virus and tracing contacts of victims was highly inefficient. It was allocated, at huge cost, to inexperienced private companies with close personal links to the Conservatives, due to the government's preference for the private sector. Boris Johnson stated in a speech to the Conservative Party conference in October 2020 that this was 'a moment when the state must stand back and let the private sector get on with it'. 'Test-and-trace' could have been managed more successfully at much lower cost by local public health departments, despite their severe cuts. The devolved governments placed greater trust in the public sector with better outcomes. From early 2021 England also used public health departments for a more intensive and effective testing service in areas experiencing new variants of the virus.[73] Throughout, as we will see, publicly funded NHS staff played the central, indispensable role of caring for Covid patients. Also from early 2021 they managed, assisted by volunteers, a very efficient system of vaccination which much reduced infection and deaths. They were widely praised and thanked.

From March 2020 the government funded 80% of the normal wages of many people temporarily unemployed due to lockdown, expecting employers to pay the remaining 20%. But many did not, to at least two million lower-paid workers. 80% of an inadequate wage increased poverty, and many low-paid and 'self-employed' workers were excluded from the scheme. UC payments were temporarily raised by £20 per week, suggesting their previous inadequacy. The exceptionally high government spending suggests the depth of the crisis. There were over six million new applicants for UC from March to October 2020, when twelve million adults and six million children were dependent upon it. Continuing deprivation is suggested by the rise in food bank use by at least 180% from March-October 2020,[74] with further growth thereafter, while homelessness kept rising. Meanwhile the rich got richer nationally and internationally, as shares and property rose in value, among other gains.

Black and Minority Ethnic communities, particularly those originating in Bangladesh and Pakistan, experienced high Covid infection and death rates, mainly because they had low incomes, worked in environments with poor protection against infection and often lived in overcrowded homes. In December 2020, 34% of Pakistani and Bangladeshi workers earned so little that they and their families were in poverty, compared with the 25% average of White families.[75] Covid made long-standing race inequalities more public, also other socio-economic inequalities, including between regions. In-work poverty was greatest in London, least in

Scotland.[76] Poverty and Covid death rates were greater in parts of Northern England and London than elsewhere. London has the richest and some of the poorest communities in the UK.

Covid also worsened and raised awareness of other social problems, including the inadequacy of social care for older and disabled people in residential homes and their own homes, and the low pay of care workers. This situation was worsened, and publicised, when the government ordered the removal into care homes of the many people occupying hospital beds who no longer needed treatment but could not find the care they needed in the community or in residential homes. They were not tested for covid before transfer and added to sickness and death rates as well as overcrowding in an already overloaded sector. Another example of official lack of concern for the needs of older and disabled people, indeed of persistent discrimination against them, was the government's slowness to provide care services with protective equipment, further raising infection and death rates among a vulnerable population. Residents suffered also from the ban on visits from family and friends during lockdown. Staff resigned due to pressure and exhaustion, causing severe staff shortages.

The NHS experienced increased demand for its services, following funding cuts and growing shortages of doctors and nurses as European immigrants left due to uncertainty about their future after Brexit, while others resigned from exhaustion and overwork. These problems, plus prioritisation of the many Covid cases, delayed treatment of other conditions including cancer and heart disease, causing further deaths. GP surgeries closed to avoid transmission of infection. Consultations were available only on-line or by telephone, leading to failure to diagnose serious conditions. Average life expectancy continued to decline, especially among the most deprived. In 2011-2018, among women in the most deprived areas of England it fell by several months to just above age 78, whereas in the least deprived it rose by several months to above 86.[77]

Nevertheless, the invaluable work of overstretched NHS staff was celebrated through the first 2020 lockdown by people throughout the UK clapping and cheering them on their doorsteps weekly. Volunteers again proved their indispensable contribution, bringing food and medical supplies to people in self-isolation, managing and contributing to food banks and much more. Even more families than before provided care for frail older and disabled relatives, including dementia sufferers, in the absence of services, often causing themselves extreme stress. The crisis also made more visible high rents, the shortage of affordable housing and cuts to local services for young people and others. Domestic violence, mental illness and suicide increased due to household lockdown and financial stress.

But Covid was not everyone's chief preoccupation in 2020. In June 2020 'Black Lives Matter' (BLM) protests spread from the US to many towns in the UK and internationally. They were sparked by the wholly unjustified killing of a Black man by police in Minneapolis, one more of many. The protests deepened anger about Black oppression more widely, including in Britain about the legacy of slavery. BLM protest in Bristol led to the toppling into the harbour of a statue of Edward Colston, one of many British men who in the past made fortunes from transporting and selling slaves. This aroused both controversy and awareness of extensive ignorance about slavery and other aspects of the history of colonialism and their possible long-term effects, leading to campaigns for improved education on these themes. There were protests also, national and international, expressing growing concerns about climate change. The Extinction Rebellion movement, founded in Britain in 2018 which then spread internationally, held large demonstrations in London and elsewhere through 2019, 2020 and later.

It remained uncertain whether the UK government had effective plans for the revival of the economy or for resolving long-term social problems revealed and deepened by the pandemic and the economic and political impact of Brexit.

Conclusion

It is difficult to summarise the path of British history since 1970 as other than one of decline. From 1945, for the first time in peacetime, the country experienced near full employment and generally rising living standards and an exceptionally supportive welfare state, which reached its peak of provision in the later 1970s. Poverty was not abolished but income inequalities shrank to their lowest recorded levels in the 1970s, and welfare benefits and services provided a 'safety net' protecting people on the lowest incomes from destitution. From 1979 income inequalities grew persistently while state welfare was undermined and poverty reached levels not seen since the beginning of the twentieth century, with similar causes. The change was the work of successive Conservative governments, ameliorated temporarily and incompletely by New Labour from 1997-2008. The economy persistently struggled as Britain's traditional strength in manufacturing declined and was not replaced and Conservative governments failed to follow Labour's lead in investing in new technology and improving skills. Young people's aspirations were affected in direct ways as well.

Income is not the only form of inequality in Britain. Housing quality, work security, educational opportunities and pensionable pay are others. There were campaigns from the 1970s for equal rights for women, gay people, minority ethnic groups, disabled people, later for older people. They all achieved gradual improvements, more from Labour than Conservative governments. Regional inequalities increased, especially due to the decline of manufacturing and mining. They stimulated the nationalist movements in Wales and Scotland leading to devolution, while in England the North/South divide continued, though it is often forgotten that London, much stereotyped as wealthy, condescending and ignorant about poor regions, contains some of Britain's greatest inequalities between rich and poor and between White people and its large population of people of colour. All have consequences for inequalities.

The differences between the two leading political parties created another central theme of the period. While some historians have perceived 'consensus' between the parties from 1945 to the 1970s (though many have not) the division between them on most areas of policy from the 1970s is undisputed. Surprising is the failure of Labour to achieve more electoral success as welfare was cut back, initially at a time in the 1980s when Social Democracy continued to flourish in France and Germany. Blair's governments achieved large majorities and improvements to welfare but felt the need to signal a degree of consensus with the Conservatives, especially by restraining public spending and playing down the redistributive effects of their policies. These attempts to appeal to 'Middle England' alienated many working-class voters who felt neglected and abstained from voting. Also, Labour was undermined by the unpopularity of Blair's foreign policies, then by the international financial crisis of 2008-2010 for which it bore no responsibility, despite the blame heaped upon it by the Conservatives, against which Labour leaders were surprisingly reluctant to defend themselves. From the 1970s right-wing neoliberalism spread strongly internationally and by the end of the century left-wing parties were weakening throughout Europe. In Britain it influenced not only politics but a large section of the press which became, and remained, stridently hostile to Labour. In the early twentieth century its influence was matched then outstripped by that of social media, whose pervasive, complex political influence remains to be analysed.

Internationally Britain continued to live up to Dean Acheson's warning in 1962 that it had 'lost an Empire but has not found a role', often dependent on alliance with the US. The successor to the Empire, the Commonwealth, remained a unique voluntary alliance of politically and culturally diverse independent states, which grew in size to the current number of 56 as states which had never been British colonies joined. But it is not obvious that it boosted Britain's international standing. Increasingly member states have withdrawn from rule by the British monarch, who headed only 16 Commonwealth states by 2022, and it was no longer led by Britain but by its members and the independent secretary-general. Britain remained a member of the UN Security Council and of the G7 and G20 but it is not clear that it exerted much influence. As a member of the EEC/EU its influence rose and fell according to the attitudes of successive premiers, but after it left in 2020 there was little sign that Britain had found another role or grown in international standing as Brexiteers persisted in proclaiming.

ADDITIONAL READING

For a more detailed account of much of the content of this volume, with full references, see relevant chapters of P. Thane *Divided Kingdom. A History of Britain, 1900 to the Present* (Cambridge, 2018).

On the **Economy**: R. Floud, J. Humphries, P. Johnson eds, *The Cambridge Economic History of Modern Britain, Vol. 2 1870 to the Present* (Cambridge, 2014)

On **Wales**: K. O. Morgan, *Revolution to Devolution. Reflections on Welsh Democracy* (Cardiff, 2015)

On **Scotland**: T. M. Devine, *The Scottish Nation, 1799-2007. A Modern History* (London, 2012), Richard Finlay, *Scottish Nationalism. History, Ideology and the Question of Independence* (London, 2022)

On **Empire, Commonwealth and Decolonisation**: Bernard Porter, *The Lion's Share: A History of British Imperialism, 1850 to the Present* (6th edition, London, 2020)

On the **Conservative Party**: T. Bale, *The Conservative Party since 1945. The Drivers of Party Change* (Oxford, 2012)

REFERENCES

[1] Estimate as 2021 Census deferred in Scotland to 2022 because of Covid.

[2] L. Black, H. Pemberton and P. Thane eds *Reassessing 1970s Britain* (Manchester, 2013)

[3] Robert Saunders, *Yes to Europe! The 1975 Referendum and Seventies Britain* (Cambridge, 2018)

[4] R. Roberts, *When Britain Went Bust. The 1976 IMF Crisis* (London, 2016); D. Healey, *The Time of My Life* (London 1989), p. 432

[5] B. Abel-Smith and P. Townsend, *The Poor and the Poorest* (London 1965); P. Thane and R. Davidson, *The Child Poverty Action Group, 1965-2015* (London, 2016)

[6] A. H. Halsey and J. Webb eds *Twentieth Century Social Trends* (London, 2000), p.479

[7] A. Beckett, *When the Lights Went Out. What Really Happened in Britain in the Seventies* (London, 2009), p. 420

[8] D. Stedman Jones, *Masters of the Universe. Hayek, Friedman and the Birth of Neoliberal Politics* (Princeton, 2012)

[9] N. Thomlinson, *Race, Ethnicity and the Women's Movement in England, 1968-1993* (London, 2016)

[10] H. Cook, *The Long Sexual Revolution. English Women, Sex and Contraception, 1800-1975* (Oxford, 2004)

[11] P. Thane and T. Evans, *Sinners? Scroungers? Saints? Unmarried Motherhood in Twentieth Century England* (Oxford, 2012)

[12] N. Kimber, 'Race and Equality' in P. Thane ed. *Unequal Britain. Equalities in Britain since 1945* (London, 2010), pp. 29-52

[13] M. Porter, 'Gypsies and Travellers' in Thane, *Unequal Britain,* pp. 71-104

[14] Results of Devolution Referendums (1979 & 1997) (parliament.uk) Table 5 - accessed 10 February 2023

[15] Ian Gazeley, *Poverty in Britain, 1900-1965* (London, 2003), pp. 65-128

[16] Eric. J. Evans, *Thatcher and Thatcherism* (3rd edition, London, 2013), p. 118

[17] M. Thatcher, *The Downing St Years* (London, 1993), p. 8

[18] P. Bew and G. Gillespie, *Northern Ireland. A Chronology of the Troubles 1968-1999* (London, 1999)

[19] P. Townsend and N. Davidson eds *The Black Report* (London, 1982)

[20] Thane and Evans, *Sinners?*, pp. 169-194

[21] D. Kynaston, *The City of London. Vol. 4, A Club No More, 1945-2000* (London, 2001)

[22] Kimber, 'Race and Equality', p. 40

[23] Porter, 'Gypsies and Travellers', pp. 84-88

[24] Helpful overviews of Thatcher's Premiership are: E.J. Evans, *Thatcher and Thatcherism* (3rd edition, London, 2013); R. Vinen, *Thatcher's Britain. The Political and Social Upheaval of the 1980s* (2nd edition, London 2010)

[25] H. Glennerster, *British Social Policy since 1945* (Oxford, 1995)

[26] Kevin Theakston, 'A Permanent Revolution. The Major Government and the Civil Service' in P. Dorey ed. *The Major Premiership. Politics and Policy under John Major,1990-1997* (London, 1999)

[27] John Major, *John Major. The Autobiography* (London, 1999), pp 265-266

[28] J. Charmley, *A History of Conservative Politics since 1830* (2nd edition, London 2008), pp 242-244

[29] P. Clarke, *Hope and Glory. Britain 1900-2000* (2nd edition, London 2004)

[30] A. Holden, *Makers and Manners. Politics and Morality in Post-war Britain* (London, 2004), pp. 276-279

[31] Clarke, *Hope and Glory*, pp. 413-415

[32] Ibid. pp 413-416

[33] Bew and Gillespie, *Northern Ireland*

[34] Clarke, *Hope and Glory*, pp. 409-412

[35] Roger Mortimore and Andrew Blick eds. *Butler's British Political Facts* (London, 2018), p. 381

[36] E. Breitenbach and P. Thane eds *Women and Citizenship in Britain and Ireland in the Twentieth Century*, pp. 63-78, 189-208

[37] R. Mortimore and A Blick eds. *Butler's British Political Facts* (London 2018), p.356

[38] Bew and Gillespie, *Northern Ireland*, pp. 352ff; Clarke, *Hope and Glory*, pp 435-437

[39] M. Clarke, 'Foreign Policy' in A. Seldon ed. *Blair's Britain, 1997-2007* (Cambridge, 2007), pp. 597-605

[40] Clarke, *Hope and Glory*, pp. 438-439

[41] B. Page, 'Culture and Attitudes' in Seldon ed. *Blair's Britain*, pp 436-467

[42] M. Clarke, 'Foreign Policy'; 'Report of the Iraq Inquiry, chaired by Sir John Chilcot', 2016 https://www.gov.uk/government/publications/the-report-of-the-Iraq-inquiry published 6 July 2016

[43] I. Bache and N. Nugent, 'Europe' in Seldon ed. *Blair's Britain*, pp 529-550

[44] R.Taylor, 'New Labour, New Capitalism' in Seldon ed. *Blair's Britain*, pp 220-237

[45] A. McKnight, 'Employment. Tackling Poverty through "Work for Those Who Can"' in J. Hills and K. Stewart eds *A More Equal Society? New Labour, Poverty, Inequality and Exclusion* (Bristol, 2004), pp. 233-246

[46] A. Smithers 'Schools' in Seldon ed. *Blair's Britain*, pp 372-381

[47] J. O'Leary, 'Higher Education' in Seldon ed. *Blair's Britain*, pp 468-475

[48] T. Blair, Fabian Society pamphlet, 2002

[49] K. Stewart, 'Equality and Social Justice' in Seldon ed. *Blair's Britain*, pp. 430-435

[50] David Willetts, *The Pinch. How the Baby Boomers Took Their Children's Future- And Why They Should Give It Back* (London, 2010)

[51] J. Hills, *Good Times, Bad Times* (Bristol, 2015), pp. 145-157

[52] Thane and Davidson, *Child Poverty Action Group*, pp. 36-41

[53] R. Lowe, *The Welfare State in Britain since 1945* (3rd edition, London, 2005), pp. 428-431

[54] N. Bosanquet, 'The Health and Welfare Legacy' in Seldon ed. *Blair's Britain*, pp 392-396

[55] M. Marmot, *The Marmot Review: Fair Society, Healthy Lives. Strategic review of Health Inequalities in England* (London, 2010), pp. 45-55

[56] P. Thane, 'Older People and Equality' in Thane ed. *Unequal Britain*, pp. 7-28

[57] H. McCarthy, 'Gender Equality' in Thane ed. *Unequal Britain*, pp. 105-124

[58] M. Porter, 'Gender Identity and Sexual Orientation' in Thane *Unequal Britain*, pp. 125-162

[59] S. Spencer, 'Immigration' in Seldon ed. *Blair's Britain*, pp. 345-355; T. Burchardt, 'Selective Inclusion. Asylum Seekers and Other Marginalised Groups' in Hills and Stewart, *A More Equal Society?*, pp. 219-227

[60] Kimber, 'Race and Equality', p 41

[61] Kimber, 'Race and Equality', pp 41-47

[62] A. Seldon and G. Lodge, *Brown at 10* (London, 2011)

[63] P. Thane, 'The "Big Society" and the "Big State": Creative Tension or Crowding Out?' *Twentieth Century British History*, 2012, Vol. 23 (3), pp. 408- 429

[64] N. Timmins, *The Five Giants. A Biography of the Welfare State* (3rd edition, London 2017), p. 662

[65] M. Marmot et al, *Build Back Fairer. The Covid-19 Marmot Review. The Pandemic, Socioeconomic and Health Inequalities in England* (London 2020), pp. 15-16

[66] Peter Apps, *Show Me the Bodies. How We Let Grenfell Happen* (London, 2022)

[67] UN Human Rights Council *Visit to the United Kingdom of Great Britain and Northern Ireland* - Report of the Special Rapporteur on Extreme Poverty and Human Rights (New York, 2019)

[68] J. Cribb, A. N. Keiller, T. Waters, *Living Standards, Poverty and Inequality in the UK, 2018* (London: 2018) www.jrf.org.uk/uk-poverty-causes-costs-and-solutions. www.resolutionfoundation.org/publications/the-living-standards-audit-2018/

[69] The Trussell Trust, *End of Year Stats 2020* www.trusselltrust.org/news-and-blog/latest-stats/end-year-stats/

[70] *The Guardian* 3 Nov. 2022

[71] Amelia Gentleman, *The Windrush Betrayal. Exposing the Hostile Environment* (London, 2019)

[72] Luke Sibieta, 'The crisis in lost learning calls for a massive national policy response' Institute for Fiscal Studies 1 Feb.2021 www.ifs.org.uk/publications/152891

[73] UK Government, *Coronavirus (COVID-19) in the UK. Daily Update* 2 Feb. 2021 https://coronavirus.data.gov.uk

[74] Trussell Trust, *End of Year Stats 2020*

[75] Joseph Rowntree Foundation *UK Poverty 2020/21. The Leading Independent Report* 14 Dec. 2020, p. 26

[76] Ibid.

[77] Marmot et al, *Build Back Fairer*